PAVE THE WAY

Embracing a Life of Legacy

Torn Curtain Publishing
Wellington, New Zealand
www.torncurtainpublishing.com

ISBN Softcover 978-0-473-57476-5
ISBN EPub 978-0-473-57915-9

Cataloguing in Publishing Data
Title: Pave The Way
Author: Bruce Monk
Subjects: Christian Life, Leadership, Spiritual tools, Discipleship, Christian maturity

A copy of this title is held at the National Library of New Zealand.

PAVE THE WAY

Embracing a Life of Legacy

BRUCE MONK

Acknowledgements

I have written this book to highlight God's goodness and faithfulness in my life. The more I have reflected, I am forever thankful for the wonderful people who have influenced my life, but I am even more grateful to Jesus Christ my Saviour for His enduring love toward me. I have enjoyed the unfolding nature of the journey God prepared for me from the beginning of time and the constant challenge to apprehend the fulness of His purpose! My love for the Holy Spirit's presence has only deepened and intensified the older I have become, especially the aspects of His guiding influence, His miraculous anointing, and the revelation of the Word of God which is the foundation on which I have built my life and ministry.

My wife Helen was 'God sent' and our testimony after more than 50 years of marriage is, 'two do become one.' Thank you, Helen, for being my support and encouragement in writing this book.

Words cannot explain how much our children and grandchildren have blessed our lives. I often cite, "I am a blessed man."

As you will read in this book, my parents paid a huge price in the formative years of my life and I am indebted to them both for their sacrifice. I honour Leslie and Sybil Monk.

Some men were significant in the beginning years of my leadership journey, namely John Douglas, Marcus Goulton, and Billy Pearson. Thank you for your patience with me!

I want to acknowledge the people who have assisted me in writing this book; Vincent Mills, Pippa Henderson, and our granddaughter Ella

Paramore for designing the cover and for assisting Anya McKee, our editor from Torn Curtain Publishing.

I esteem you all highly for the gifts and grace on your lives. Be blessed!

Contents

Introduction

If I was to write a mission statement that would best describe my purpose and summarise my God-given destiny, it would have to be "to equip and empower the next generation." I gain as much delight in seeing others succeed as I do myself.

One of the motivations for writing this book is to give God praise for His amazing works, and also to declare to my children, grandchildren, and spiritual children the acts of God and His faithfulness. It has been said that in our youth we strive to *succeed*, but as we mature, something changes and we focus more on *significance*—the need to bring meaning and purpose to everything we do. Self-seeking becomes unimpressive. We realise that significance is found in carving a path for another generation to follow.

I am personally grateful for the input of many leaders, comrades, and family who have helped shape the person I have become in my journey of life and leadership. But foremost, I want to express my heartfelt gratitude to God for His direct counsel, revelation, and divine understanding He has brought to me via the Holy Spirit on a continuous basis.

To the readers of this book, my prayer is that you will be greatly inspired through the pages of my story to pick up the call of God confidently, and intentionally seek to invest into another generation as you outwork God's purposes in your own life.

PART ONE

LEGACY AND INFLUENCE

1

Establishing a Legacy

"Instead of your fathers shall be your sons, whom you shall make princes in all the earth. I will make your name to be remembered to all generations."

— PSALM 45:16-17

Life is a journey, and in its formative stages most of us are not fully aware of just how God works. Growing up in rural New Zealand, my only ambition was to follow in the gumboot-clad footsteps of my father. He was a farmer, just as his father had been, and I'm sure many generations before were also. Farming was in our blood and my early dreams centred on continuing that legacy.

My father, Lesley Earl Monk, was an exceptionally generous man, and my older brother and I were the grateful recipients. Waking early each morning, we would accompany our father to milk the herd of dairy cows, feed the livestock and tend to the farm, learning from his experience and knowledge of farming as we did. My father was determined to pass on his wisdom to ensure we had what it took to become farmers in our own right. With his support, we were well on our way to becoming established and prosperous. That support was unexpectedly disrupted, however, when our father suffered a major heart attack. He was only in his early fifties at the time. From that point on, his lifestyle changed dramatically. He could no longer endure the physical vigour that daily farm duties required, and increasingly my father handed ownership and responsibility of the farm to my brother and I, ensuring that it would continue to thrive and turn a profit.

We certainly lived in a productive region of the country. Sitting pretty at the base of the Tararua Ranges on the rugged west coast of New Zealand's North Island, is my hometown of Otaki. At the time, this rural community had a population of around three thousand people. It was known as the 'produce market' for the nation's capital, supplying milk and vegetables to the Wellington region just an hour to the south.

During my growing years, the local Brethren church in Otaki ran a club known as Every Boys Rally, which I attended every Thursday evening. I have never forgotten my initial commitment to follow Jesus. I was twelve years old, sitting on a pew amidst a gaggle of gangly, pre-pubescent boys in an old church hall. From the moment I entrusted my life to Christ, I genuinely believed in Him, and every Sunday when I attended the local Anglican Church with my parents I enjoyed declaring that belief by reciting the Apostle's Creed:

"I believe in God the Father almighty,
Maker of heaven and earth,
and in Jesus Christ, the only begotten Son of God."

At that time, however, the church had no specific discipleship programme to develop young people in their faith, character and godly values. Like many others, as I entered my young adult years, I made choices based on what felt good and what was in it for me. I was a typical young farmer.

I was nineteen when Helen and I started going out. She had first caught my eye at a carnival to raise money for a community swimming pool where she was one of the 'princesses' representing the town Surf Lifesaving community. Being a farmer, I supported the country community of course—only, our 'princess' wasn't nearly as striking as the beautiful young lady with a slight figure, dark brown eyes, long hair and soft, tender personality, standing in front of me.

Helen was two years younger than me and although she had grown up on a neighbouring farm, her parents had since moved into town where her father had established an electrical and plumbing business. The business served the farming community and he had invited me, as one of his customers, to come along to a party at their family's house. As the party began I was glad to see Helen again, but I had to be careful because one of my close friends was keen on her. Thankfully, he left the party early, I managed to catch her attention, and by the end of the night Helen was sitting on my knee. This was the beginning of our love story, but I was too insecure to be tied down in a steady relationship. After a while I broke it off, leaving Helen very hurt.

I was not fully aware of God's working in my life at the time, but that changed a couple of years later when I had a serious car accident. Driving home after drinking until the early hours of the morning, I fell asleep at the wheel and, drifting onto the opposite side of the road, collided with an oncoming car. I cannot remember the collision, but found myself waking up in hospital suffering mainly from internal injuries. While I was recovering, Helen came to visit me and our friendship was reignited. Soon after I was discharged from hospital we started going out again.

To this day I am very thankful that my life was spared and I didn't suffer any major ongoing consequences. The accident was the result of my own stupidity, yet God used it to catch hold of my heart. I vividly remember, not long after, sitting on a dirty cow trough on my father's farm reflecting on the recklessness of my choices.

By the end of that year Helen and I were engaged, and we married a year later. Why delay the inevitable?! Helen was twenty and I was twenty-two. We have never regretted marrying at a young age. Our lifelong, loving marriage (something I will reflect on later in this book) has flourished for over fifty years. Helen is the most precious gift I have ever received, and our journey together can only be described as blessed.

———

At this point in life, my brother and I were working together to operate the family farm on a shared basis with our father. There were two houses on the property, and after our engagement my father considered building a third home for Helen and I. Having always been enterprising and an opportunist, I seized the chance to share a crazy idea with my father. Instead of building a house on the existing farm, I asked if he would lend me money which I could use, along with my savings, as a deposit to buy my own farm.

Coincidentally (or miraculously), the ideal farm came onto the market around the same time. It was just south of Otaki in a small town called Te Horo which consisted of little more than a single grocery store, a garage, and an engineering workshop. The farm lay at the foothills of the beautiful Tararua ranges. Sloping towards the sea, it came with amazing views of the ocean and Kapiti Island in the distance. By New Zealand standards it wasn't a large farm—around one hundred and fifty acres—but it was lucrative.

After much discussion and consideration, my father decided to sell our home farm to my brother, thereby making it possible for both his sons to become farm owners. And so, with the help of the bank, and enabled by our father's generous heart, Helen and I began a new life chapter together. Just a few months after sharing my idea with my father, I had the joy of escorting my bride through the gate of a farm rather than over the threshold of a house, a farm that included both our names on the title deed.

What an amazing start to life for a young, newly-married couple! We quickly prospered simply because I worked hard and was excellent at what I did. My boyhood dream had become a reality, and I wasn't going to squander the opportunity that was before me.

My father continued to bless us even after we had a farm of our own. I have many fond memories of him driving out to see us with his dog in the back of his Ute, and asking me, "What can I do for you today?" He came to serve. He never said it, but he knew that a twenty-two-year-old needed direction and guidance. Through his example and the teachings of Jesus, I have come to realise that this is the greatest form of leadership. As I fondly reflect back over that early part of my life, the greatest legacy my father left me was not just financial. It was his model of servant leadership, his generosity of heart, and his willingness to make a major transition and sacrifice in order to empower the next generation.

Soon, another generation was on its way. In the first five years of our marriage, Helen and I welcomed four children into the world—Rebecca, Hamish, Samuel and James. Just as we've never regretted marrying young, we've never regretted having children so soon, or so close together. Our children have enriched and enhanced our lives in so many ways and have always been an important part of everything we have done.

Sadly, my father passed away when he was just fifty-nine but before he died, both he and my mother became followers of Jesus Christ. They were baptised in water and in the Holy Spirit. My mother, Sybil, went on to live a further thirty-seven years after the passing of my father. She was ninety-seven when she passed, and through her unconditional love and acceptance, she too left an amazing legacy for our family and the many others who met her.

Just before my dad died, however, the Holy Spirit began stirring our hearts to something new. Helen and I started feeling a call on our lives to leave farming and become full-time ministers. We had been attending a very small Pentecostal church which was part of the Apostolic movement (now called ACTS Churches). At that time, the church didn't have a full-time pastor, so I was often given the opportunity to lead and preach. Every time I spoke, the call to ministry intensified and my love for farming began to dwindle. An undeniable desire to become a pastor had started to take its place.

Our vision was tested, however, when an ideal opportunity arose to purchase another farm. This farm not only had an established dairy unit, but came with beef and sheep units as well! After viewing the property I was certain we could also make it work financially. This was the epitome of my boyhood dreams! But as I drove home, I felt intuitively in my spirit that while buying this farm would have been okay, this wasn't God's destiny for our lives. And so, guided by Psalm 119:105, Helen and I walked away from the opportunity and soon after, made the decision to employ a manager for our farm so that I could attend Bible College for a year. The light of God's word into our lives had illuminated our future and set us on a road that would transform me from a farmer into a pastor.

"Your word is a lamp to my feet and a light to my path."

— PSALM 119:105

The decision to leave the farm changed the direction of our lives forever. Within a few years, we sold our farm so we could completely embrace God's calling for our lives. I often wonder how my father would have handled such a radical decision. He was a wonderful father to me in terms of care and generosity, but God also used him to establish a guiding principle that has had a major impact on my life and ministry ever since:

"Live to leave a legacy!"

My father maximised what he had, and later traded it to ensure both his sons were firmly planted into a solid future. One farm became two. One generation passed a more expansive legacy to the next.

This pattern of building on what we are originally entrusted with in order to leave a legacy is a principle that has defined our life. As with my father, it has taken humility, sacrifice, and an intergenerational mindset. Legacy wonderfully increases in scope when it is stewarded well.

For Helen and I, leaving an intergenerational spiritual legacy has been central to our thinking over many years. It has guided us in our major life-decisions and been at the heart of strategic choices that we now look back on with contentment and joy. With a legacy mindset we can embrace significant loss and change, knowing that God is paving the way for increased levels of fruitfulness in our lives and in the lives of others.

2

Embrace an Emerging Generation

"One generation shall praise Your works to another, and shall declare Your mighty acts."

— Psalm 145:4

My year at Bible College was pivotal. Under the guidance and investment of leaders with strong apostolic giftings, the call on my own life was soon recognised, and at the end of that year I was formally ordained and credentialled as a pastor in the Apostolic movement. From there, I took up a role as an assistant pastor for one year. This was a time of development as I outworked what I had learned at Bible College, implemented programmes, and learned to listen to God's directives in the context of leadership and ministry.

As that year came to an end, we heard about a church in the city of Whanganui that had by all accounts 'died out' and had recently closed. With faith in our hearts and high expectation in the Spirit, Helen and I put up our hands for the task of reopening the church in that city.

I was twenty-nine years old when we arrived in Whanganui with four very young children and a caravan in tow. Finding no houses available to rent, we settled into a caravan park for the summer, where the children could make the most of the swimming pool and be enrolled in the local school until we could find a suitable house.

At the time, Whanganui's population of about forty thousand was comprised of two extremes—families with historical wealth on one hand, and labourers on the other. The main industries were meat works, wool processing plants and agricultural machinery production. However, what the people delighted to inform us about their city, was that it had the reputation of being a preachers' graveyard—not the most encouraging welcome for a couple of inexperienced leaders!

Although my year of studies had given me a basic education in theology, hermeneutics, preaching, and an Old Testament and New Testament survey, Helen and I were thrown in the deep end when it came to leadership and church life. Consequently, Whanganui became an important training ground for us both. My library grew at a fast pace as I consumed books on leadership, biblical understanding, church growth and structure, and revival, along with biographies of great leaders and missionaries. Helen excelled in her ability to gather people, hosting significant events for children, women and married couples, and bringing many people into increased levels of freedom. Together we attended conferences and courses and gleaned ministry tips from old cassette tapes. We were passionate, not only to learn and develop in our role, but also to minister in the power of the Holy Spirit to those God was bringing into our lives.

Over the next eight years, the young church in Whanganui experienced steady growth. This was accompanied by powerful testimonies of salvation and miraculous healings. One young mother who had newly committed her life to Christ had a son who suffered with severe eczema on his arms and legs. This young boy was consistently wrapped in bandages and, because of the constant irritation, he would scratch this skin relentlessly to the point of drawing blood. At his mother's request, we anointed him with oil and prayed a prayer of faith. Within two days, she called to say the eczema was disappearing, and by the following Sunday there was no trace of eczema on his body!

The combined testimonies of the mother's salvation and the boy's healing caused people's faith to increase and word soon spread that Jesus was "present in the house to heal!" In turn, our faith grew and our leadership was established in this church, for which we are continually thankful. In this season we also discovered the importance of prayer and fasting, and as we pursued those disciplines our conviction, confidence and courage were strengthened.

Our early leadership years were distinguished by a determination to focus on the next generation. Helen developed creative children's programmes that took place in the middle of the week and on Sundays. The impact was two-fold—not only did our own children love being in these environments, but it served as a very effective ministry to our community. Our home soon became a hub for children. It resounded with happy noise—and incredibly high volumes of it too! Initially our children attended both services on Sundays, and it wasn't uncommon to find them asleep under the seats by the end of the evening service.

I must say, leading a church while also being responsible parents was intense. So, to take care of our own emotional health, we engaged a babysitter one night a week for a period of time. Helen and I loved this arrangement and it was certainly worthwhile in terms of our wellbeing. We had one night a week to ourselves! Later in life we learned that the moment the children heard the garage door rise, they rushed to their beds so when we entered the house everything appeared calm. We always just assumed they were fast asleep. Great memories!

———

The formative years of our lives are vital. In Whanganui we were growing at a fast pace in many areas. Juggling the tension between family and ministry required our constant attention, and we wanted to ensure that our children would not suffer through the busyness of our lives. We wanted to develop sustainability and an identity as a family unit, so we built in fun activities, set aside special family times, and made sure we planned great holidays. Eventually, that purposeful combination of rest and living life purposefully became 'just what we do' as a family.

Knowing we are loved by a God that never changes helps establish our identity. It allows us to feel secure and steady in our day-to-day activities, while vision keeps us moving forward. If I was to describe this in one sentence, I would say, "When we are defined by God's love, we are drawn by His purpose."

A scripture that has helped me in gaining a greater understanding of my purpose is Psalm 144. There, King David writes:

> "Rescue me and deliver me from the hand of foreigners, whose mouth speaks lying words, and whose right hand is a right hand of falsehood—that our sons may be as plants grown up in their youth; that our daughters may be as pillars, sculptured in palace style; that our barns may be full, supplying all kinds of produce; that our sheep may bring forth thousands and ten thousands in our fields; that our oxen may be well laden; that there be no breaking in or going out; that there be no outcry in our streets. Happy are the people who are in such a state; happy are the people whose God is the Lord!"
>
> — PSALM 144:11-15

Through my father's wonderful example of building legacy for the next generation and my own experience of entering fatherhood, this scripture came with fresh revelation to my heart, enabling me to acknowledge that God was writing a more expansive script for the future.

This became a focal point throughout our ministry in Whanganui.

With a legacy-perspective solidified in my mind, I knew from the outset that our focus would be on the emerging generation, and when we later moved to New Zealand's largest city to pastor the church known today as Equippers Church Auckland, we took with us an even greater vision for a creative children's ministry, a dynamic youth and young adult ministry, relevant music, and the establishment of a bible college.

Legacy was a significant consideration when, in the year 2000, Helen and I received clear direction to move to London to establish a church. By then the church in Auckland had grown to around one thousand people, with a bible college and campuses for a Creative Learning School which focused on teaching young people who had poor records of school attendance. The big question we had to grapple with at that time was who would take over the senior leadership of the Auckland church.

After much prayer and discussion with the elders, along with the national leaders of our movement, it was decided we would appoint Sam Monk, our third child. Sam was just twenty-six years old, and given his age, this was a big risk. But as I prayed, the Holy Spirit reminded me of the step my father had taken in entrusting the responsibility of a farm to me when I was only twenty-two. Sam had already built a significant young adults ministry from zero to over two hundred young adults. He had also given important leadership to our creative team through a period of transition.

And so, towards the end of the year 2000, Helen and I went to London on a three-month trial period and Sam was officially commissioned as the senior pastor of the Auckland church, of which I would still maintain apostolic oversight. This began a new journey of discovery and learning for Sam, while Helen and I were being used by God to create a platform of ministry that continues to have an impact in London and throughout Europe today. On the other side of obedience is God's blessing!

Sam has now led the Auckland church for a longer period than I did before him, and it has gone from strength to strength. His gift of leadership has grown and flourished beyond his years. His wife, Kathy, has also shown how women can find a secure place in God's house, becoming everything God has called them to be. As the Psalmist wrote,

> "Our sons . . . (are) as plants grown up in their youth . . . our
> daughters . . . as pillars, sculptured in palace style."
>
> — PSALM 144:12

To release another generation into leadership, we who are fathers must also embrace our calling. The closing verses of the Old Testament prophecy strongly regarding what happens when fathers fail to take their place:

> "Behold, I will send you Elijah the prophet before the coming
> of the great and dreadful day of the Lord. And he will turn
> the hearts of the fathers to the children, and the hearts of
> the children to their fathers, lest I come and strike the earth
> with a curse."
>
> — MALACHI 4:5-6

It's interesting that the last verses of the Old Testament carry a warning and stress the importance of preparing and empowering the next generation. We have observed that when people in positions of leadership do not empower another generation of leaders, the younger generation are prevented from finding their place. Many organisations struggle because they are remiss in addressing the tension that potentially exists between the generations, and fail to implement the necessary adjustments.

Our experience has shown us that young people are the energy of the church (or any growing organization) and, given good leadership and spiritual covering, they are able to carry weight and responsibility incredibly well! We can also testify that when we empower the next generation we build a platform for the growth of the church.

Our society has done a good job of identifying the problem of fatherlessness, but has failed to address some of the root causes. As a result, young people are crying out for fathers who will not only believe in them, but lovingly address the issues that hold them back in life and ministry. They long for fathers to create an environment where they can be equipped to outwork and achieve the God-given dreams they carry.

A fatherless society emerges when fathers are consumed with their own interests and thus fail to prepare the next generation to take a firm hold of their future. As a result, just like Malachi prophesied, the earth is struck with a curse. The church must lead in this area! As the church, we have what it takes to turn back the massive wave of insecurity that is crashing down upon our modern-day society with a vengeance. The Apostle Paul identified this problem in his day when he wrote,

"For though you might have ten thousand instructors in Christ, yet you do not have many fathers; for in Christ Jesus I have begotten you through the gospel."
— 1 CORINTHIANS 4:15

Having instructors who educate us is important, but education alone cannot replace the security that comes from fathers whose hearts are turned to the children. It is through effective nurturing that the next generation are able to steward their God-given gifts to places of maturity. A person who is not nurtured often becomes insecure and unsteady in life, tends to live without boundaries, and is more vulnerable to failure, often resulting in irreparable damage to themselves and others.

The following are key characteristics that I consider to be important in fathers:

- Fathers help young people discover their God-given gifts, and create an environment for equipping, training, and development.

- Fathers should understand the importance of pressure for the formation of strength within a young person. Therefore, they shouldn't attempt to remove or divert the pressure from the next generation unless they sense it's becoming destructive or dangerous.

- Fathers shouldn't always tell people what to do but instead help them to 'dig their own well' and 'find their own spring'.

- Fathers must give room for younger people to fail or make mistakes without condemnation, knowing that this is how they learn to make adjustments and succeed.

- Fathers should have as much joy in seeing others succeed as when they succeed themselves.

- Fathers need to understand the importance of building for the next generation, and value the biblical pattern of passing a blessing from one generation to another.

What a legacy this perspective brings. The answer lies in the heart of the fathers! When the hearts of the fathers make the first move, the hearts of the children can soar. These days, the biggest compliment anyone can give me is to say, "Bruce lives to inspire the next generation."

3

Embrace Growth

By our eighth year in Whanganui the church had grown both numerically and in health, and we had begun to engage in discussions about the exciting possibility of relocating to Auckland. When our leadership asked us instead to take up responsibility for a church in the Wellington region, we were initially disappointed but chose to honour that request and submit to their oversight.

The focus in Lower Hutt, Wellington, was to see renewal in a church that was dwindling, to invest in the next generation, and to stay true to our identity as loved children of God. It was a season of special significance for our family, with all of our children baptised both in water and in the Holy Spirit during that time. Not only that, the church, though small in numbers when we took it on, experienced a great move of the Holy Spirit and the congregation soon tripled in size! Within just ten months of investing into the Lower Hutt church, we were commissioned to our next pastorate—this time, in Auckland.

Auckland was a city God had been laying on our hearts for some time, and we approached the move with anticipation. However, when we arrived, we were inducted into a church that had lost its way. Having been part of the Apostolic movement that had its origin in the Welsh revival, this church had certainly known seasons of success. We were aware when we accepted the appointment that the church was in need of reformation, but we had not yet seen the church building or met the people we would be leading.

When Helen and I took over, we could immediately see that this church was tired. With no clear vision to reach out to the community or see souls saved, it existed only to lift up the flag of the movement. Only thirty-five people attended, six of whom were retired pastors and their spouses! To add to the difficulty of the situation, the movement had recently purchased a new building for the congregation—a former Jehovah's Witness hall on the very outskirts of the CBD.

I had an immediate dislike of the building the moment we entered it. Usually, I am an optimist—I look for the possibilities—but I knew something was wrong, not only with the building, but with the location. Our vision had been to establish a multicultural church in the inner city with a particular focus on reaching an emerging generation. This was important for us personally because our children were all in, or approaching, their teenage years.

As leaders, we must stay sensitive and true to what God has placed in our spirit, and no matter how I tried, I just couldn't find peace, or see this location as part of our future. And so, within our first year, we secured a community hall in the central city for our Sunday services. We then sold the original complex, which ultimately set us up to buy one of the oldest theatres in the city—a venue with a seating capacity of five hundred and fifty.

We were now at peace, knowing we were being true to the vision God had given us. Our new premises enabled rapid growth. Following the Sunday morning service, the youth would often gather in a nearby park for a game of touch rugby. After the evening service, Helen and I would buy hot fries, a few loaves of bread, tomato sauce and some bottles of Coca-Cola, and invite the youth back to our home, where they would hang out and play music with the volume turned right up. I often wondered if the youth were coming to church simply because of the dinner afterwards, but it was encouraging to see how these simple gatherings helped impact our children, and it was these evenings that became a strategic part of growing our church.

Many years ago, I read an article stating that eighty-five percent of people make a commitment to Christ before the age of twenty-five. This has proven accurate in my experience. I have been in services all around the world where I have asked people to stand if they committed their lives to follow Jesus Christ before the age of twenty-five, and without exception around eighty-five percent of the congregation stand. From my observation, most churches struggle because they cater primarily to the other fifteen percent—those who came to Christ later in life, or transferred from other churches. Churches that make the emerging generation their focus, however, usually enjoy a thriving church culture as well as steady numerical growth.

This was certainly true during the first years of the Auckland church. With five hundred people regularly attending, I was thankful for the lives that were being reached and transformed as a result of the church's ministry. And yet I experienced a growing frustration. I sensed we had hit a ceiling, only I had no idea what that ceiling was.

———

By now, I had been in ministry for almost twenty years. I had reformed and planted successful churches across New Zealand, and Helen and I were well overdue for a sabbatical. That year, we took two months off and decided to travel. We visited Australia, South Africa, Burkino Faso, London, New York and Hawaii, followed by a sixteen-day bus tour through France, Switzerland, Italy, Austria, Germany, Netherlands and back to London. We certainly covered a lot of ground and saw some wonderful sights! I can't say I especially enjoyed being herded from one place to another, but even so, we returned home feeling refreshed and challenged for the next phase of our ministry.

It was soon after arriving back home that the Holy Spirit challenged me one day during my devotions to make this scripture a prayer for my life:

"And God gave Solomon **wisdom** and exceedingly **great understanding**, and **largeness of heart** like the sand on the seashore."

— 1 KINGS 4:29

This verse drew my attention to something that would be essential to my capacity and ability to invest in future generations. It also highlighted my own limitations. I knew I could gain increased wisdom and understanding through intentional reading, attending seminars, and associating with people who were further along the path than I was. But the challenge to cultivate *largeness of heart* was a new concept for me. The more I prayed, the more I came to the conclusion that the ceiling I had hit—the limiting factor in taking the church to another level—was actually me!

I had never thought of myself as having a small heart, but obviously God saw it differently. *Largeness of heart like the sand on the seashore.* I often went for walks by the sea, but even then, my imagination could not begin to grasp the extent to which every grain of sand represented a person. Then one morning, as I was walking along the beach, I was reminded of the time when Jesus encountered a man with a withered arm. Jesus commanded him to stretch out his arm, and immediately it was healed (Matthew 12:9-13).

In faith, I stretched out my arm. It was a prophetic action, a picture of what I believed the Holy Spirit was doing in my heart. I was declaring to my future that I was growing in my capacity to love. Later that morning while I was praying in my office, I experienced a powerful encounter with the Lord. I had just read the words of Psalm 78:40-41:

"How often they provoked Him in the wilderness, and grieved Him in the desert! Yes, again and again they tempted God, and limited the Holy One of Israel."

In that moment I found myself caught up into heaven, standing in the presence of Jesus Christ. Naturally, I was in awe of His presence. Then He said to me, "Bruce, I have never doubted your love for Me, but while you were on earth you limited Me. I wanted to accomplish far more through your life." From that moment on, my perception was transformed and I started to dream bigger. God was enlarging my heart, and my life could not remain the same.

———

My clarity of vision, conviction, and strategic capacity quickly started to increase, along with the apostolic grace upon my life. I developed a strong impression that God was calling me to plant ten churches in ten major cities of the world. Through subsequent encounters with God, the Holy Spirit showed me how to proceed with the vision.

The first step was to position the Auckland church to increase its soul-winning capacity by opening our hearts to reach the nations in global missions. As a result we changed our missions focus as a church. Up to that point, our "missions department" focussed on supporting missionaries in different countries. Now we shifted our approach, enabling the church as a whole to operate as a family on a mission together, reproducing ourselves through planting churches. We began reaching beyond our own country by sending a couple to commence a church plant in London. Fourteen years later, Helen and I also embraced the challenge, relocating to England in order to pick up where they left off.

The London church grew slowly but steadily, and with many young adults from nearby universities joining in, Equippers London was soon well established. Not long after we arrived in London, the Senior Minister of Hillsong London, Gary Clarke, gave me an important prophetic word. The essence of that word was that God had primarily called me to London to be a father who would raise up significant leaders, and that it would be these leaders that would bring the growth.

Over time, that word came to fruition as God brought together strategic people, many of them young adults who subsequently took on major leadership roles and are still an integral part of Equippers' ministry around the world. Today, Equippers Church has an influential apostolic house in London that impacts nations throughout Europe and beyond. I am forever thankful for the wonderful people God has brought into our lives over the years—those who not only caught the vision, but willingly took hold of the challenge to reproduce the culture of what was to become the Equippers Network.

My approach in the early years of our ministry was to establish a large, strong church in Auckland that would empower others to reach out and plant churches. This was the model I had studied and observed in other influential churches. I had gleaned a lot through reading, listening to messages, attending conferences, and visiting churches like Hillsong in Sydney, Willow Creek in Chicago, Kensington Temple in London and Abundant Life in Bradford, England. At this stage in my ministry, however, the Holy Spirit was showing me a different plan. My new primary focus would be to raise up an apostolic company of leaders, and for that, I needed to become flexible and mobile. We also needed to stay focussed on equipping and empowering the next generation.

I became increasingly aware that God had called Helen and I to hold our own unique direction and not become an imitation of something else. Just as an original painting can command a much larger price than a replica, God wanted to bring His unique fingerprint to the initiatives He was about to establish through our lives and the churches we would go on to plant.

Many leaders of ministries and churches are aware of the prophetic vision God has entrusted to them, and those that have lasting impact seek to walk the vision out in a contemporary setting. They are aware of the times and seasons they live in. Over the years, I had fought the temptation to be intimidated by the success of others. This is essential to grasp because if we are living under the umbrella of a competitive spirit, feeling constantly threatened by the success of others, we cannot thrive and will always feel inferior.

I was becoming increasingly aware that the Holy Spirit wanted me to push the 'refresh button' on what I had been taught, and to rediscover some of the truths that had been suppressed through tradition and institutionalism. This was the beginning of a long journey as I sought to find answers to difficult questions, and grappled to uncover what would best serve a vision for the future and empower the next generation. In Ephesians 2 Paul writes:

"Now, therefore, you are no longer strangers and foreigners, but fellow citizens with the saints and members of the household of God, having been built on the foundation of apostles and prophets, Jesus Christ Himself being the chief cornerstone, in whom the whole building, being fitted together, grows into a holy temple for the Lord, in whom you also are being built together for a dwelling place of God in the Spirit."

— EPHESIANS 2:19-22

The Apostle Paul's vision for the local church was clear—he identified the importance of the ministry of apostles and prophets in establishing the foundation and the prophetic pattern the Holy Spirit has for the Church. This was fulfilled by the original apostles Jesus appointed, but it is also a framework for the church today. Christ remains the chief cornerstone, and Paul emphasised the importance of building in reference to Him. Leadership must stay true to that blueprint; we cannot be swayed by denominational traditions or the expectations of others. The kind of leadership Paul articulated has an important role in establishing the beliefs, culture, vision, and mission of every emerging church and ministry.

Upon reflection, I have come to identify some key areas that help to grow capacity and amplify our legacy.

We must:

1. Possess a confident belief in the Holy Spirit to inspire vision and impart conviction for a bigger tomorrow. This will help prevent us from limiting God.

2. Acknowledge that God's blessing is on the other side of our obedience. The importance of obedience in order to defeat the enemy is seen in Psalm 81:13-14: "Oh, that My people would listen to Me, that Israel would walk in My ways! I would soon subdue their enemies, and turn My hand against their adversaries."

3. Resist being distracted by opposing voices and views. A powerful example of this is found in Nehemiah 4:1-6 where a constant stream of opposing voices only served to strengthen Nehemiah's resolve, spurring him on to do the work that God had placed on his heart.

4. Allow pressure and opposition to increase your capacity. Throughout the Bible we learn the lessons and value of pressure. One account is in James 1:2-4: "My brethren, count it all joy when you fall into various trials, knowing that the testing of your faith produces patience. But let patience have its perfect work, that you may be perfect and complete, lacking nothing."

5. Empower others to carry responsibility. Jesus called the twelve apostles to be with Him, and ultimately, they would carry His vision of His kingdom to the known world.

6. Learn how to let money serve the vision and not become the master that controls. Jesus said in Matthew 6:24, "No one can serve two masters; for either he will hate the one and love the other, or else he will be loyal to the one and despise the other. You cannot serve God and mammon."

7. Trust God to keep working even while we sleep. We need to do our part and leave the rest to Him. Psalm 37:5 says, "Commit your way to the Lord, trust also in Him, and He shall bring it to pass." I have often prayed, "Help me get better at trusting You, Lord," and have learned that the more I trust God, the greater impact and influence He will have through my life.

PART TWO

HEALTHY TRANSITIONS

4

Embrace Change

Generally speaking, Helen and I have been good at transitions and embracing the next season. What has helped us is understanding that life works in seven-year cycles. At the start of a cycle, everything is new. We are growing and developing into our new role. By the fifth year, we normally have found our stride and are starting to enjoy the fruit of our efforts. As the seventh year approaches, however, things can become predictable to the point where we are no longer being stretched.

As a couple we have always found that the Holy Spirit prepares us at the right time for the next season. Over the years, I have learned to identify when a season is changing. The main indicator is that I tend to fall back into managing what is, rather than initiating something new, meaning my faith is not engaged at the same level as when I first entered that season.

Far too many leaders have an elevated view of their own importance, often holding attitudes of entitlement, and carrying prophetic revelation that has not been tested by other leaders. When we transitioned the leadership of the Auckland church to our son, Sam, we needed to extract ourselves from many natural and emotional securities. The Auckland church graciously supported us financially so we were free to go to London, but we needed to let go of the security that came through having a fixed salary and some of the extra benefits that accompanied this. On an emotional level, we had been pastoring the church for fourteen years, and many of our relationships had been forged through the highs and lows of life during that time. We had officiated at weddings, dedicated children, counselled people through difficulties, and led the church through the purchase of buildings and the establishment of a bible college and programmes that reached into the needs of our city. And yet we found that the pain associated with letting go of something that was already succeeding was lessened because our focus had already shifted to embrace a new vision and direction. For us, it was the faith adventure of commencing a church in London.

Transitions can be difficult, but the courage that is needed to cross over into the next season of ministry or life keeps our connection with Jesus alive, and our faith strong. One of the main reasons people don't cross over is concern for financial security. Even though this is valid, it doesn't justify leaders holding onto a current position and thereby hindering another generation from taking their place. Emotional security is another reason some people find it very difficult to extract themselves from leadership positions. This is why many leaders find themselves lonely and feeling rejected when they retire. In the end, we are all stewards, and whatever God entrusts to us we must hold lightly.

It is helpful to consider Jesus' prayer as He approached the most significant turning point in His ministry. Soon he would give His life for the world, and with His sacrifice an era of unstoppable kingdom expansion was set in motion. In John 17:1-5 we read,

> "Jesus spoke these words, lifted up His eyes to heaven, and said:
> 'Father, the hour has come. Glorify Your Son, that Your Son also
> may glorify You, as You have given Him authority over all flesh,
> that He should give eternal life to as many as You have given
> Him. And this is eternal life, that they may know You, the only
> true God, and Jesus Christ whom You have sent. I have glorified

You on the earth. I have finished the work which You have given
Me to do. And now, O Father, glorify Me together with Yourself,
with the glory which I had with You before the world was.'"

The prayer of Jesus at this pivotal moment highlights important questions
for each of us in our own ministry or life transitions:

WHO FILLS YOUR VISION?

Jesus was about to face the cross. He could have been consumed with His
own needs, but instead we read, "He lifted His eyes towards heaven, and
said, 'Father'" (John 17:1).

I once heard a preacher tell the story of his travels in Africa. As they
journeyed, their tour group came across a herd of elephants. He asked
the driver to stop for a moment so he could take a photo. Holding the
camera at arm's length, he sought to capture himself in the photo with the
elephants in the background. Quickly he returned to the waiting vehicle
and they departed. As they proceeded down the road, the preacher opened
his camera to view the photo, only to find that the frame was completely
filled with an image of his own head, a grey background, and the elephants
nowhere in sight!

If our worldview consists of a frame filled only with an image of ourselves,
our ability to accomplish lasting kingdom outcomes through our lives will
be limited. Our worldview needs to be bigger than our own needs. In the
same chapter we read Jesus' words:

"I pray for them. I do not pray for the world but for those whom
You have given Me, for they are Yours. And all Mine are Yours,
and Yours are Mine . . ."

— John 17:9-10

Like Jesus, we need a greater view of our lives; we need heavenly perspective. Jesus understood that His life's purpose was eternal. In John 18:37 He said, "For this cause I was born, and for this cause I have come into the world, that I should bear witness to the truth."

HOW BIG IS YOUR FAITH?

As He faced a transition in His ministry, Jesus had no problem asking the Father to glorify Him. This was because the motivation of His heart was to bring glory and honour to His Father through His actions and life. In prayer He said:

> "Father, the hour has come. Glorify Your Son, that Your Son also may glorify You."
>
> — JOHN 17:1

The glory of God is attractive, and like Jesus, we must carry it in increasing measure through each of life's transitions. In His death, Jesus demonstrated to the world the greatest act of love known to mankind, and in so doing revealed God's glory as He, by faith, laid hold of His Father's purpose for His life. Likewise, we display God's glory when we reach out with mercy, minister in the spirit, extend forgiveness, give godly wisdom, walk a life of righteousness, demonstrate Holy Spirit-anointed power and strength, and reflect Christ in every aspect of our lives. As we reach beyond our comfort zone and step into a new season, we position ourselves for the glory of the Lord to be manifested through us, and our faith grows significantly as a result.

The Holy Spirit is calling us to interact with Him in our walk of faith so we will grow into the likeness of Jesus Christ. This happens when we, by faith, respond to the Holy Spirit's quickening and embrace the Word of God. I like the way Paul describes this in his second letter to the Corinthians:

"But we all, with unveiled face, beholding in a mirror the glory of the Lord, are being transformed into the same image from glory to glory, just as by the Spirit of the Lord."

— 2 Corinthians 3:18

From the beginning, God's image was flawlessly displayed in humanity. But when sin came in, that image was marred. As a result, we all grow up struggling to find our true identity. When we look into the mirror of our life, we see an image that is broken, cracked, clouded, and even has missing sections. This is why we struggle with insecurity, fear, pride, and arrogance. For some people, their soul is constantly bent over and buckled because of hereditary patterns that have been transferred from one generation to another. But as we look into the mirror of God's Word we see, not our imperfections, but the image of Christ, and thus we are transformed 'from glory to glory'. It is essential, then, in times of change, that we invite and empower the Holy Spirit to adjust not only our direction or focus, but also our lives.

I am a very passionate person and often found, as I approached seasons of change, that I tended to develop a short fuse, sparking outbursts of anger. Of course, Helen didn't like these outbursts, and she challenged me about it on many occasions. But more often than not, I brushed it away by entertaining the thought, "This is who I am." One day, however, Helen said, "Bruce, I can't take any more of your anger." This time, I took her words more seriously. The next morning while I was having my devotions, I reflected on her words, and I heard God speak into my spirit, "Neither can I." Helen's words had provoked me to think, but having God on my case provoked me to change. This is how the Holy Spirit works! He changes us from glory to glory *by the Spirit of the Lord.*

The reality is that transitions and change bring fresh adventure but also fresh pressures. As our own shortcomings rise to the surface, this is not reason to cower, or ignore what is going on in our hearts. It's a time to embrace internal change as well. I was grateful when our church network announced they had scheduled time for each of our New Zealand pastors to meet with a psychologist. Helen and I took the opportunity, and as we sat with the psychologist, I began to describe the short fuse I had developed, and my desire to mature in that area. With insight and grace, this man traced the pattern of our lives, relating accurately to us our projected responses in any given situation. While Helen was described as a 'flat liner' in regard to her personal needs, he explained that with the level of passion I possessed, it could only have been by God's grace that I hadn't burnt out already. That response affirmed to me the way God had wired me, while prompting me to ask for fresh help. "God," I prayed, "You've got to help me get control of my angry outbursts."

And He did. I understood that repentance is not simply remorse—it is a deliberate mindset that allows us to gain the victory over sin and be increasingly transformed into the image of Christ. Whenever I felt anger rise up, I chose in repent. Over time, my tendency to anger grew weaker. Yes, there are moments of power to be had in prayer, but ultimately, we as God's people are *gradually transformed.* We are changed *from glory to glory.* From glory, to glory—not condemnation!

When we respond to challenges by being changed into the likeness of Christ, our faith grows. In turn, the Holy Spirit enables us to minister in the power and the glory of God. We need big faith; we need to ask that God would grant us *His* glory! God longs for a generation that will wholeheartedly live to glorify Jesus Christ in every area of their lives. God will not give His glory to another, but He will entrust us with His glory when we, like Jesus, simply pray, "Glorify your son, that your son also may glorify you" (John 17:1).

DO YOU KNOW YOUR AUTHORITY?

Jesus was confident in the authority that was entrusted to Him by His Father. In His prayer, we read, "You have given Him authority over all flesh" (John 17:2). Jesus said something similar to His disciples in John 14:12-14:

> "Most assuredly I say to you, he who believes in Me, the works that I do he will do also; and greater works than these he will do, because I go to the Father. And whatever you ask in My name, that I will do, that the Father may be glorified in the Son. If you ask anything in My name, I will do it."

Jesus Christ has given us authority to rule and reign with Him! As Christians, we remain powerless until we realise the extent of the God-given authority entrusted to us through the name of our Lord Jesus Christ. Two key scriptures make this very clear. In Matthew 16:19, Jesus said:

> "And I will give you the keys of the kingdom of heaven, and whatever you bind on earth will be bound in heaven, and whatever you loose on earth will be loosed in heaven."

Then in 1 John 5:14-15 we read:

> "Now this is the confidence that we have in Him, that if we ask anything according to His will, He hears us. And if we know that He hears us, whatever we ask, we know that we have the petitions that we have asked of Him."

One of my first attempts at exercising this God-given authority happened when I was running my dairy farm. I went through a difficult season when many of my stock were dying. The veterinarian who visited my farm declared that another animal would die by the end of the day. In my absolute frustration I slapped my hand on the back of the cow and declared, "In the name of Jesus, stand up!" To my amazement she did, and she recovered immediately! I did not lose any more stock from that point.

Prayer and godly authority are not old-fashioned religious acts practiced by a few faithful servants. They're used by those who know how to usher in the kingdom of God. Unlike trends that come and go, they are timeless and powerful tools. If there was ever a time for Christians to arise, to harness the power of prayer, and exercise godly authority, it is now. Paul writes:

"For the kingdom of God is not in word but in power."
— 1 CORINTHIANS 4:20

Prayer is an action that brings God's kingdom power to earth. To access the presence of God boldly requires confidence and faith, knowing that He hears us. As God calls you to take new steps of faith, He also calls you to rise into your authority in Christ!

IS YOUR LIFE FILLED WITH MISSION AND GODLY PURPOSE?

Jesus' prayer shows us that He lived beyond this current world. He lived with an eternal perspective! Jesus' mission, quite simply, was to make the Father known.

"And this is eternal life, that they may know You, the only true God, and Jesus Christ whom You have sent."
— JOHN 17:3

As I think of all those who have stepped out in faith, motivated by mission and godly purpose, I can't help but think of the parable of the Good Samaritan in Luke 10:25-37. There Jesus highlights the importance of taking responsibility for broken humanity by laying aside our religious prejudice and social pride, and lending a hand to those in need.

Many years ago our youth pastor at Equippers Church Auckland came to me with real concern for some of the young people who had started to attend church but were not going to school. They were truants, and even the police were finding it difficult to deal with them.

We agreed to start a learning programme for these youth, and we called it the Creative Learning Scheme. The school was initially sponsored by the church and I admit we faced some enormous challenges until the government eventually provided some assistance. But there were other issues too—for one, the neighbours were not happy about a group of young truants venturing onto their street every day. Despite this we persisted, and today thousands of young people have grown and benefited, even going on to higher education, through this simple response to a need.

Mission must be at the heart of every church and every child of God. As we grow in maturity, we need to be continually open to the need around us, bringing purposeful and practical responses. As we do so, God is able to creatively frame and shape how He will enlarge our usefulness.

This is why Equippers has become a church 'on mission' rather than simply a church with a missions department. Mission is at the center of who we are! As a movement we are committed to:

- Proclaiming the gospel of Jesus Christ. Every week we witness people responding to the gospel and giving their hearts to Him.
- Equipping people for life through faith in Jesus Christ by helping them lay hold of God's purpose for their lives.
- Planting life-giving churches that reproduce a culture of mission.
- Walking out our faith and becoming channels of the Holy Spirit's anointing and power.
- Reaching out to broken humanity with loving acts of help and service.

I am sure we are all guilty at times of brushing past the very people the Holy Spirit is calling us to reach out to. But when we, like Jesus, take an eternal view of life, we are working for a lasting reward that will never be taken from us.

WHAT LEGACY DO YOU PLAN TO LEAVE?

We are inspired by the life and ministry of Jesus Christ, and His death and resurrection is central to our personal salvation. But in John 17, we see that Jesus was primarily concerned about the legacy He would leave through the men who had been entrusted to Him. As He embraced the journey to the cross, Jesus knew the ongoing ministry of the kingdom of God was about to rest with these men and their willingness to yield to the Holy Spirit for the cause of Christ.

We see this reflected in the words of His prayer:

"I have glorified You on the earth, I have finished the work which You have given Me to do."

—JOHN 17:4

What legacy did Jesus leave behind? It is true that He impacted the world at large more than any other person, and that His death on the cross and triumphant resurrection changed the course of history. But John 17 is a prayer for those whom the Father had given to Him, and there we catch a glimpse of His heart for legacy:

"I have manifest Your name to the men whom you have given Me out of the world. They were Yours, You gave them to Me, and they have kept your Word" (v. 6).

I am often inspired and motivated by the testimonies of men and women of faith that have gone before, especially those described in Hebrews 12:1-2:

"Therefore we also, since we are surrounded by so great a cloud of witnesses, let us lay aside every weight, and sin which so easily ensnares us, and let us run with endurance the race that is set before us, looking unto Jesus, the author and finisher of our faith, who for the joy that was set before Him endured the cross, despising the shame, and has sat down at the right hand of the throne of God."

As we consider our life's work, may we be those who can look around with confidence and witness another generation that has been inspired through our lives to run in faith and pick up the baton that the Holy Spirit is passing to them. When I come to the end of my life, I pray that I too will be able to stand and declare, "I have finished the work You have given me to do."

5

Embrace Prophetic Direction

A prophetic generation does not accept current reality but lives with spiritual insight, dispelling fear, destroying insecurity, reaching out to create a better future, and trusting God to move on their behalf. As we embrace prophetic direction we position ourselves for greater impact, prophetically shaping the generations that follow.

Not long after graduating from Bible College I received the same prophetic word through five individuals in five different locations over a period of just two months! The word was a direct quotation from Proverbs 3:5-6:

> "Trust in the Lord with all your heart, and lean not on your own understanding; in all your ways acknowledge Him, and he shall direct your paths."

Because it was a direct quotation from the Bible, my initial response was to ignore it as a prophetic word. But by the fifth time it was spoken over me, I realised God was wanting to get my attention. Looking back over my life now, I can see that one of my greatest struggles has been to simply trust Him. My temptation has been to lean towards human reason and understanding. But I have learned that sometimes God creates ambiguous situations simply so that we might learn to trust Him! At the beginning of my ministry, my preference was for everything to be clearly laid out for me. Because I am logical in nature, I needed the assurance that every step was planned before I made a move. My life was like a holiday without any allowance for downtime. There was little room for spontaneity—until I learned that the Holy Spirit doesn't work this way. He prophetically inspires us with a vision of the future, and then leads us *step by step.*

Just as John the Baptist was called by God to prepare the way for the first coming of Christ, the Holy Spirit is raising up a prophetic generation to prepare the way for His second coming. This generation will be marked by their passion to see Christ's kingdom established on earth as it is in heaven. They will have hearts of humility, trust, and dependence on God. They will walk in the confidence, courage and boldness that comes from living with a prophetic vision of the future and a sincere passion for the cause of Christ.

Being captivated by something bigger than our current reality keeps our lives filled with purpose. My dream has long been to equip and mobilise the next generation so they can come to a place of maturity beyond their years and prophetically lay hold of their future. We have learned to find ways to impart wisdom—even in today's context where technological advances see young people able to effortlessly access information yet they increasingly struggle with loneliness and a lack of purpose.

Interestingly, studies have shown that the more time we spend on social media, the more likely we are to feel lonely. In other words, the less social media, the better the social life! Renowned researcher, Jean Twenge, observed a shocking rise in psychological health issues among the generation who first reached adolescence after the introduction of smartphones. This generation demonstrated a higher percentage of depression, suicide, eating disorders, homesickness, and above all, anxiety, than in any prior generation.

The church today has a responsibility to fill the void created by the rise of technology and inspire another generation of youth with a prophetic cause. We need to teach them how to manage the tension between their current reality and a God-breathed future. This future has an appointed time, and we must allow the Holy Spirit to first prepare us so that in turn we may be able to prepare others.

I see God raising up an army of young people who will live for the cause of Christ and take the gospel of salvation to the world. We must resist the tendency to create a consumer attitude to Christianity instead of inspiring people with the Great Commission. We need to replace messages that create an attitude of "what's in it for me?" with the call to "take up your cross and follow Christ."

This is why we must cultivate churches that truly embrace being 'on mission' together rather than defaulting to a worn and weathered model of missions. Mission is not necessarily about going overseas. It is a compelling desire to lay hold of Christ for the reason He has laid hold of us. Paul sets the example in Philippians 3:12-14:

> "Not that I have already attained, or am already perfected; but I press on, that I may lay hold of that for which Christ Jesus has also laid hold of me. Brethren, I do not count myself to have apprehended; but one thing I do, forgetting those things which are behind and reaching forward to those things which are ahead, I press toward the goal for the prize of the upward call of God in Christ Jesus."

Paul wrote these words in the latter part of his life—some commentaries say he was in his mid to late sixties—yet he had not lost sight of his prophetic vision.

To this day I am thankful for the prophetic words spoken over my life by faithful men and women. Even as a young man with very little biblical understanding, someone spoke of the apostolic call upon my life. In the early years of my ministry a prophet told me that I would be able to quickly catch the heart of an emerging generation of leaders, and equip and release them. Yet another man declared there would come a season in my life when my bags would virtually never be unpacked. Over recent years this has been my reality, and I have travelled outside New Zealand for close to six months of every year.

There have been many words spoken over me calling me a reformer, especially in terms of helping reposition church movements for fresh seasons of growth and expansion. One prophetic word said I would go from nation to nation, leaving a footprint in each nation upon which leaders would stand and establish great works of God. I am now seeing this word fulfilled before my eyes. Together, Helen and I have established Equippers churches in fifteen nations, and every one of them is now led by a national of that country. What a testimony of God's faithfulness in bringing His prophetic word to pass!

The key to living in line with our calling, then, is to hold onto prophetic directives. These words determine the impact of our lives. John the Baptist modelled this powerfully when he apprehended the prophetic direction to "prepare the way of the Lord" (Mark 1:3).

Rather than calling those words into question he embraced them, and in so doing, positioned a generation for the coming of Jesus. He was secure in his mission because of the prophetic word!

In Ephesians 1:15-23 the Apostle Paul wrote:

"Therefore I also, after I heard of your faith in the Lord Jesus and your love for all the saints, do not cease to give thanks for you, making mention of you in my prayers: that the God of our Lord Jesus Christ, the Father of glory, may give to you the spirit of wisdom and revelation in the knowledge of Him, the eyes of your understanding being enlightened; that you may know what is the hope of His calling, what are the riches of the glory of His inheritance in the saints, and what is the exceeding greatness of

His power toward us who believe, according to the working of His mighty power."

His prayer was that we, the church, would embrace the prophetic word and operate with the same level of security and conviction about our mission.

UNDERSTAND PROPHETIC DESTINY

Our future is shaped by the voice of the Holy Spirit, the Word of God, prophetic words, and the counsel of others. When these are working together, we find that the peace of God becomes the umpire of our heart. It is a peace beyond human understanding. I love how the Bible encourages everyone to seek Him and declares that if we are sincere in our quest, we will find Him (Proverbs 8:17, Jeremiah 29:13, Matthew 7:8).

As we take steps toward our dreams, it is important to guard our hearts against discouragement, and resist any temptation to become offended along the way. A dream or vision has a time appointed to it, and the Holy Spirit is committed to the task of preparing us for the job at hand. The story of Joseph (Genesis 37-50) is a powerful illustration of keeping one's spirit strong even when the circumstances are contrary. Joseph was a dreamer, but sadly his vivid dreams provoked his brothers to anger, and they ended up betraying him. He was falsely accused by his boss's wife and imprisoned. Yet through all this, he maintained a positive attitude of hope that allowed him to prosper. At the right time, he found himself standing, not only in his dream, but in God's ordained position for his life.

UNDERSTAND PROPHETIC DECLARATION

As we navigate change, it is essential that our words align with God's Word. This is often very difficult to maintain, especially when we are confronted with opposing circumstances. There will be seasons when our faith is tested and the dreams in our hearts appear very distant.

However, when we draw near to God, He promises to draw near to us. As He dispels our fears and lifts us above despair and unbelief, we come away renewed, and are enabled, with a clear sound, to declare God's Word into our circumstances.

I have learned that prophesying God's Word can usher in a change of season. In the Bible, Ezekiel is instructed by God to prophesy to the dry bones of a dead generation as they lay in a valley.

> "So I prophesied as I was commanded; and as I prophesied, there was a noise, and suddenly a rattling; and the bones came together, bone to bone. Indeed, as I looked, the sinews and the flesh came upon them, and the skin covered them over; but there was no breath in them. Also He said to me, 'Prophesy to the breath, prophesy, son of man, and say to the breath, "Thus says the Lord God: 'Come from the four winds, O breath, and breathe on these slain, that they may live.'" So I prophesied as He commanded me, and breath came into them, and they lived, and stood upon their feet, an exceedingly great army."
>
> — EZEKIEL 37:7-10

I am praying that we too will be a people who do not *fear* death, but instead *rattle* death by speaking God's prophetic word into lifeless circumstances! It's time to disturb death itself, speaking God's Word over a new generation and empowering them to rise up and lay hold of God's purpose for their lives.

UNDERSTAND PROPHETIC ACTION

God's blessings lie on the other side of our obedience. Many people have good intentions but remain disconnected from blessing simply because they rationalise away what God has said and refuse to obey His Word.

When my mother was in her late eighties, Helen and I received the word that we should go to London. At the time, my mother was disappointed by our decision to leave New Zealand, but we chose to obey what God had spoken. When we returned from London seven years later, my mother was still alive and was able to celebrate what God had done throughout our time in London. I have often thought that if we had succumbed to her emotional need rather than clinging to God's word for our lives, we would not have seen what the Holy Spirit released and is still outworking as a result of that one deliberate act of obedience.

In Psalm 81, Asaph explains in a couple of sentences a theme that is woven right through the Bible—that God will deal with the enemy if we will simply obey Him.

> "Oh, that My people would listen to Me, that Israel would walk in My ways! I would soon subdue their enemies, and turn My hand against their adversaries."
>
> — PSALM 81:13-14

Then in Revelation, John speaks of three ways we defeat the enemy:

> "And they overcame him **by the blood of the Lamb** and **by the word of their testimony**, and they **did not love their lives to the death**."
>
> — REVELATION 12:11

This third phrase is essential to grasp. If we are to leave a legacy that extends beyond ourselves, we must be prepared to 'lose our lives' for the sake of Christ (Matthew 16:25). The Bible speaks of denying ourselves, choosing instead to follow the leading of the Spirit. Our obedience sets a platform for the Holy Spirit to work on His prophetic word!

UNDERSTAND PROPHETIC REACH

Many years ago during an Air New Zealand flight, I was glancing through the onboard magazine when I was captivated by a map showing Auckland as a significant transit hub with flight paths extending out from that city to touch many nations of the world. I instantly saw a vision of Equippers Church Auckland becoming a hub for training and equipping, with people eventually being placed into the bow of the Holy Spirit and fired like arrows into the nations of the world. In outworking this vision, Isaiah 19 became a strategic scripture:

> "And He has made My mouth like a sharp sword; in the shadow
> of His hand He has hidden Me, and made Me a polished shaft; in
> His quiver He has hidden Me."
>
> — ISAIAH 19:2

This verse encapsulates God's prophetic direction for the Equippers Network. The verses that follow primarily refer to the mission of the coming Messiah, but the Holy Spirit used them to spark a prophetic vision for our churches and outline our mission as His covenant people:

> "Thus says the Lord: In an acceptable time I have heard You, and in
> the day of salvation I have helped You; I will preserve you and give
> You as a covenant to the people, to restore the earth, to cause them
> to inherit the desolate heritages; that You may say to the prisoners,
> 'Go forth,' and to those who are in darkness, 'Show yourselves'"
>
> — ISAIAH 49:8-9

For many years, the Auckland church held a corporate prayer meeting every Wednesday evening using the scripture in Isaiah 49 as the foundation for our praying:

I give you (accepting God's mandate for us as a church)
as a covenant to the people (embracing the gifts given to us)
to restore the earth, (ministering to see restoration and healing)
to cause them to inherit, (releasing a godly inheritance)
to say, go forth, and show yourself (reflecting God's glory in our
generation).

Today, we can testify to God answering those prayers! One of my greatest joys is to see people lifted by the power of redemption out of bondage and difficult circumstances. It brings me so much joy to see people who come from backgrounds of generational curses—poverty, addictions, sexual obsessions, depression, and oppression—being set free, cleansed by Christ, and propelled into a brighter future! I love hearing of young married couples buying their first home even in the face of growing house prices. When we embrace what God speaks regarding us as individuals and as churches, we see families, communities and nations transformed by His goodness.

A PROPHETIC GENERATION UNDERSTANDS THE PROPHETIC VOICE

Proverbs 18:21 states that life and death are in the power of the tongue. It is important that a prophetic generation knows how to tame the tongue and speak words of life. Many years ago, I felt personally challenged by Ephesians 4:29:

"Let no corrupt word proceed out of your mouth, but what
is good for necessary edification, that it may impart grace to
the hearers."

This scripture came as a rebuke to me because I had found myself attracted to negative conversations. Many a move of God has been robbed of its full outworking by personal ambition, jealousy, discord, and pride—all hiding behind a mask of spirituality and cloaked in unedifying, discouraging words. When I was challenged by this scripture in Ephesians, I asked the Holy Spirit to help me change my language so that my words would impart grace. I must say that over the years, it has been a challenge to bridle the tongue! However, the words of Jesus compel us to consider the weight of our own words:

> "For assuredly, I say to you, whoever says to this mountain, 'Be removed and be cast into the sea,' and does not doubt in his heart, but believes that those things he says will be done, he will have whatever he says. Therefore I say to you, whatever things you ask when you pray, believe that you receive them, and you will have them."
>
> — MARK 11:23-24

Jesus left us with the challenge of aligning our faith with the confession of our mouth, thereby becoming a prophetic voice in a world where fear is increasing and hopelessness is robbing people daily of emotional wellbeing. As we partner with Him through the words we speak, we release restoration to a hurting world.

6

Embrace Prayer

As a young man I was taught the importance of prayer, but my knowledge of how and what to pray was definitely lacking. With good intentions, I would kneel down to pray, only to find myself waking up in a very uncomfortable position! From this place of frustration, I found the Lord's Prayer a helpful place to begin. In Matthew 6, Jesus said,

> "In this manner, therefore, pray:
> Our Father in heaven,
> Hallowed be Your name.
> Your kingdom come.
> Your will be done on earth as it is in heaven.
> Give us this day our daily bread.
> And forgive us our debts,
> As we forgive our debtors.
> And do not lead us into temptation,
> But deliver us from the evil one.
> For Yours is the kingdom
> and the power and the glory forever. Amen."

"In this manner" can be also translated, 'in this way,' or 'according to this pattern,' or even 'pray like this.' I have no problem repeating the words as they were written, and this was very much part of my experience growing up as a member of the Anglican Church. But as I searched for ways to develop my prayer life, I started to use the Lord's prayer as a pattern rather than as a rote prayer.

I divided the prayer into six sections, and by doing this my engagement increased and my 'prayer muscle' got stronger. Sometimes when I am out walking I will concentrate on each aspect of the Lord's prayer for about two minutes, usually praying with a sense of purpose and direction for a total of about twelve minutes. This approach can enable us to redeem time while walking, driving, or engaging in activities that don't demand mental energy.

Our father in heaven, hallowed be Your name.

Some years ago, I heard Shane Willard speak on this verse. He mentioned that a more accurate way of interpreting this line would be, "Our Father, in the air I breathe, I stop and remember You." I like this, because heaven is everywhere, and praise is an intentional response that lifts us from our current circumstances, allowing us to stop and remember Him.

Psalm 100 instructs us to "Enter into his gates with thanksgiving, and into His courts with praise." Likewise, in Isaiah 61:3 we are encouraged to:

"... (put on) the garment of praise for the spirit of heaviness."

Many people are attracted to meditative worship, yet this is not a style that requires our souls or attitude to come intentionally and purposefully before the throne of grace. In contrast, choosing praise and thanksgiving is a deliberate decision to leave our current position and to seek to position ourselves where Christ is, rather than attempting to bring Christ down into our predicaments.

To help me rise beyond my current thought patterns and develop praise-centred language, I often turn to the psalms. For example, Psalm 34 is an expression of the blessings that come to those who trust God:

"I will bless the LORD at all times;

His praise shall continually be in my mouth.

My soul shall make its boast in the LORD;

The humble shall hear of it and be glad.

Oh, magnify the LORD with me,

And let us exalt His name together.

I sought the LORD, and He heard me,

And delivered me from all my fears."

— PSALM 34:1-4

This expression of praise comes from the lips of King David. It speaks of lifting our heart in praise, but psalms such as this can also help us when we are facing negative emotions, opposition, or fear on our journey of life. As we take the words and make them our own, we find that turning scripture into prayer becomes a powerful tool. The psalms, in particular, give expression to all of our human emotions and provide language that turns our focus heavenward.

Your kingdom come. Your will be done on earth as it is in heaven.

From my observation, this is one of the most quoted parts of the Lord's Prayer. I like to link this phrase with the words of Jesus in Matthew 16:19 when I am praying through this section:

"And I will give you the keys of the kingdom of heaven, and whatever you bind on earth will be bound in heaven, and whatever you loose on earth will be loosed in heaven."

— MATTHEW 16:19

Jesus has given us the authority to rule and reign with Him. In this section, I regularly pray by name for all of my family, including my twelve grandchildren. I have prophetic statements for all of them, declaring God's kingdom rule in their lives. This is also when I pray for others, for our church, for God's kingdom expansion around the world, for more leaders, and for our government and godly leadership in our nation. It is also the time when I stand against the works of evil and bind negative influences so that the power of the Holy Spirit can be released. One of the advantages of being older is that one can testify to God's faithfulness and answered prayer over many years!

Give us this day our daily bread.

God's provision covers many aspects of our lives. Naturally, we need finances to survive in a modern world, and it is important to pray for God's provision in this area. Helen and I have many powerful testimonies of God's financial blessing, especially as we have moved through different seasons of transition. I also like to pray for God's provision of physical strength, for His supply of supernatural grace, for the food of His Word to nourish my soul and keep me in health, and for His provision of wisdom and understanding. Over the past two years I have begun regularly praying through Isaiah 40:31:

> "But those who wait on the Lord shall renew their strength; they shall mount up with wings like eagles, they shall run and not be weary, they shall walk and not faint."

This scripture has taken on a new meaning as I have prayed through each aspect of it:

- Waiting is not being idle, but rather involves allowing God's will to be woven together with our will and coming into agreement with Him so that He in turn can bring strength to our lives.

- Mounting up with wings like an eagle means positioning ourselves to see as God sees, bringing greater insight and clarity of vision to our current circumstances.

- To run and not be weary is about being empowered to accomplish God's full purpose for us. Weariness is a curse that robs people from the joy of serving.

- To walk and not faint is about having the strength of faith and conviction not to give in or give up. In a busy world, we need the provision of God's grace and strength.

These prayers take our lives from the natural realm into the supernatural realm. It's my belief that this is where God has designed us to live, because this is where we learn to trust Him. Psalm 37:3-4 says, "Trust in the Lord, and do good; dwell in the land, and feed on His faithfulness. Delight yourself also in the Lord, and He shall give you the desires of your heart."

Forgive us our debts as we forgive our debtors.

Recently I returned to the area where I grew up, and took the opportunity to visit the location where I was baptised when I was in my early twenties. Earlier I mentioned the serious car accident I experienced back in Otaki while driving home in the early hours of the morning under the influence of alcohol. The accident is a blur to me because I had fallen asleep at the wheel before veering onto the other side of the road and colliding with an oncoming car. To this day, I am so thankful that no one in the other car was killed. I was lucky to come out in good shape too—scarred only by the guilt and shame which I carried. But on my baptism, as I was submerged below the water, the guilt and shame dissolved, and my heart was overwhelmed with God's love and forgiveness.

The Christian journey is filled with encouragement that springs from our relationship with the Holy Spirit, our faith in God's Word, and the victories we find in Christ through His Word. But there are still moments when we yield to the weakness of our humanity. When I come to this section in prayer, I am reminded to keep a short account with God; to keep my heart free from any offence, and to release people from my judgement. Every one of us will struggle with offences at different points in our journey with Christ. I have found freedom when I have forgiven those who have offended me and returned blessing to them, even if I've felt I have been wronged.

> "For if you forgive men their trespasses, your heavenly Father will also forgive you. But if you do not forgive men their trespasses, neither will your Father forgive your trespasses."
>
> — MATTHEW 6:14-15

Living free and at peace are amazing blessings that overflow from living a life in harmony with our Creator!

Do not lead us into temptation, but deliver us from the evil one.

One of my spare time activities is fishing. I mainly fish with a rod, and these days I use biodegradable lures. The idea of a lure is very much like the so-called 'carrot' that the enemy of our soul dangles in front of us to tempt us as he seeks to draw us away from our path of victory and freedom. This pattern is explained clearly in James 1:12-15:

> "Blessed is the man who endures temptation; for when he has been approved, he will receive the crown of life which the Lord has promised to those who love Him. Let no one say when he is tempted, 'I am tempted by God'; for God cannot be tempted by evil, nor does He Himself tempt anyone. But each one is tempted when he is drawn away by his own desires and enticed. Then, when desire has conceived, it gives birth to sin; and sin, when it is full-grown, brings forth death."

Temptation never disappears, but the Holy Spirit can empower us to live above it so that we don't yield or take a bite of the bait that is often very subtly cast before us.

"No temptation has overtaken you except such as is common to man; but God is faithful, who will not allow you to be tempted beyond what you are able, but with the temptation will also make the way of escape, that you may be able to bear it."

— 1 CORINTHIANS 10:13

When we understand how the enemy operates and what is at stake in our own lives and churches, we begin to see the power of praying this regularly: "Do not lead us into temptation, but deliver us from the evil one."

Yours is the kingdom and the power and the glory.

The Lord's Prayer begins by setting our focus on magnifying God and exalting His powerful name. It finishes by returning our acknowledgement to Him for His kingdom reign, His power, and His glory. Prayer is about ruling and reigning with Christ. How wonderful it is to lay your head on the pillow at night and say, "While I sleep, I am thankful, and acknowledge Your power, Holy Spirit, to keep working on my behalf." This deals with those anxious moments, when we lie awake trying to solve the world's problems.

I want to conclude this chapter by asking you to pray this blessing over your life in the name of our Lord and Saviour Jesus Christ. It comes from Numbers 6:23-26:

"This is the way you shall bless the children of Israel.
Say to them:
'The Lord bless you and keep you;
The Lord make His face shine upon you,
And be gracious to you;
The Lord lift up His countenance upon you,
And give you peace.'"

PART THREE

DISTINCTIVES AND IDENTITY

7

Embrace Vision

"I purpose to build a house for the name of the Lord my God,
as the Lord spoke to my father, saying, 'Your son, whom I
will set on your throne in your place, he shall build the house
for my name.'"

— 1 KINGS 5:5

David passed on to Solomon, his son, a God-inspired vision to build a house for God because David was unable to complete it in his lifetime.

God builds generationally, and the example given in this story must inspire us to do the same. Sadly, God's purpose and the cause of Christ are often hamstrung because the senior leadership of churches tend to stay in positions beyond their use-by date. I am constantly amazed by the language that is used to justify that position. Attitudes of entitlement, unrealistic expectations of one's own abilities, prophetic revelation that remains untested by other leaders, isolation, and a lack of trust in God to provide are common factors that hinder the kingdom of God from advancing.

It is inspiring when vision and the purpose of God can flow from one generation to another. In the story of David and Solomon, the latter had a willingness to embrace the vision God had entrusted to his father. Reading through the life of David in the book of 1 Samuel, we see that David had won the necessary battles, defeating the enemy, and creating an environment of peace that freed Solomon to build a house for God.

As I mentioned previously, our third child, Samuel, became the senior pastor of the Auckland church when Helen and I went to London. I must admit how pleasantly surprised I was when everyone embraced the proposal to transition the leadership of the church to our son. As time progressed Sam did face some major challenges, which is to be expected, but one of the powerful testimonies that people constantly shared with me was how seamless the transfer of leadership actually was. One of the reasons for this is that we had imparted clear vision to the next generation. As well, Helen and I both continued to hold an apostolic, overseeing role in the church, and I remained on the eldership. In the years that have followed Sam has openly embraced our input, and continues to establish the progressive vision God has for the church while also adding his own strength and flavour of leadership.

CLARITY OF MISSION AND VALUES RESULTS IN SEAMLESS TRANSITIONS

A major reason the Auckland church enjoyed a seamless leadership transition was the way in which Samuel embraced of the overall mission of the church and embodied the cultural values that had been outworked over many years. Early on, Sam attended many of the DNA classes that I taught to people who wanted to make the Auckland church their home church. Then he gradually began teaching portions of this course. Looking back, it wasn't long before Sam had taken complete ownership of this. The values of the church had become his values, and therefore, like Solomon and David, it became easy for him to continue building the dream God had placed in our hearts for the Auckland church and beyond.

When Sam became the senior pastor, the church was called Auckland City Church. With our move to London, however, we decide to rename it Equippers Church because of the clear mandate upon our lives to equip and empower another generation. We had already formed the Equippers Network International (ENI) in New Zealand. ENI had become a thriving and effective gathering of ministers, the focus being "to add value to churches and leaders."

The change of name of the Auckland church was a natural but significant step. We had already established an Equippers Church in London that was built upon the same values as the Auckland church and carried the same mission statement: "Equipping people for life through faith in Jesus Christ." The feel of both churches soon became very similar. This is true now of Equippers churches around the world. Even though they function in different languages, these churches all have a similar atmosphere because we share the same mission; each church has adopted the same values, which help us build together. In terms of legacy, this is key. When building a church (or anything, for that matter), many people do not have clarity about what they are building and can therefore be easily swept up in the latest fad or craze. If the next generation is to find their place, we must communicate clarity of vision, values, and purpose.

Because David built generationally, Solomon was able to bring his gifts of grace to the building of a temple that ultimately would attract the attention of their known world. Even today, we are reaping the benefits of Solomon's wisdom and understanding, a legacy he established because he not only feared God but had the humility of heart to build upon the platform created by his father, David.

CLARITY OF VISION RESULTS IN DECISIVE LEADERSHIP

The Bible contains many powerful passages about the need for vision and the importance of living with godly purpose. The one that has had the greatest impact on my life is found in the gospel of Mark. There, Jesus is approaching the end of His earthly mission. He has just entered Jerusalem on a donkey and been welcomed with an anthem of singing and loud praises. Then, in Mark 11:11, we read that Jesus went into Jerusalem and into the temple, and "when He had looked around at all things, as the hour was already late, He went out to Bethany with the twelve."

Notice that Jesus surveyed the situation before going to Bethany to sleep. There is no information about what took place that night, but the next day Jesus acted decisively in response to what He had seen. We read:

> "So they came to Jerusalem. Then Jesus went into the temple and began to drive out those who bought and sold in the temple, and overturned the tables of the money changers and the seats of those who sold doves. And He would not allow anyone to carry wares through the temple. Then He taught, saying to them, 'Is it not written, "My house shall be called a house of prayer for all nations?" But you have made it a den of thieves.'"
>
> — MARK 11:15-17

Jesus' indignation over the contradiction between His vision for His Father's house and the reality of what he witnessed in the temple was warranted. His vision declared, "My house shall be called a house of prayer for all nations" (Mark 11:17). Hence, His authority to lead and act as He did arose from what He had first observed.

Taking the time to gain a full perspective of the situations we encounter allows us to act in a considered manner rather than to impulsively react in the moment. This is why establishing clear vision is vital. When the vision is clear and our values are defined, those who lead are empowered to act decisively and establish boundaries so their vision will not be compromised.

We have seen this play out in the area of worship. Early in ministry we declared a vision to establish a church for the emerging generation. One of the ways we facilitate that is through our choice of worship style. When Christians join our church and ask why we don't sing old hymns, or wonder why we don't have prolonged worship, we can give a reason without being condemning. Because our vision is clear, we don't feel compelled to compromise it to accommodate other preferences. Decisive leadership enables us to stay true to the vision, and the authority to 'overturn tables' and 'drive out' that which doesn't belong in the context comes from being absolutely clear on what we are building.

CLARITY OF VISION RESULTS IN GROWTH

Initially, our vision was to establish ten 'apostolic houses' (resource churches) in ten significant cities around the world. We saw these churches built with the same conviction of mission: having a secure foundation of belief and adopting values that can extend from one country to another. From these churches, we would see multiplication taking place. God has been faithful and we have now surpassed ten churches, which we always envisioned being closely aligned in mission and values.

There have been many moves of God that have impacted nations around the world while their vision to extend the kingdom of God and their unique values were fresh. Over time, however, many of those God-inspired initiatives became institutionalised and therefore lost their power to impact and change the world as they did in the beginning. The structures we build must serve the vision we have been entrusted with. The moment the vision of a movement becomes controlled by the structure or the institution, it becomes a slippery slope, with the leaders often finding themselves losing their original gains. This is why we need God-appointed and anointed leadership that constantly challenge the current structure to ensure it serves God's plan and purpose.

CLARITY OF EXAMPLE RESULTS IN ANOINTED PATTERNS

Looking back at the story of Jesus' visit to the temple, we can see how the temple leadership lost sight of God's original plan. The temple was to be a place that would host the presence of God. It was to be a house of worship and prayer, and a place where the scriptures were taught, but it had been compromised to the point where it existed only for the benefit of man rather than to glorify God. Godly traditions had been set in institutionalism and religious duty rather than through Holy Spirit-anointed leadership that focussed people lives towards the Creator of the universe.

Earlier in His life, when Jesus visited the synagogue just after returning in the power of the Holy Spirit from the wilderness where He had been tested for forty days, He quoted a scripture from Isaiah 61:1-2. We read:

> "So He came to Nazareth, where He had been brought up. And as His custom was, He went into the synagogue on the Sabbath day, and stood up to read. And He was handed the book of the prophet Isaiah. And when He had opened the book, He found the place where it was written:
> *'The Spirit of the LORD is upon Me,*
> *Because He has anointed Me*
> *to preach the gospel to the poor;*
> *He has sent Me to heal the brokenhearted,*
> *To proclaim liberty to the captives*
> *And recovery of sight to the blind,*
> *To set at liberty those who are oppressed;*
> *To proclaim the acceptable year of the LORD.'*

Then He closed the book, and gave it back to the attendant
and sat down. And the eyes of all who were in the synagogue
were fixed on Him. And He began to say to them, 'Today this
Scripture is fulfilled in your hearing.' So all bore witness to Him,
and marvelled at the gracious words which proceeded out of His
mouth. And they said, 'Is this not Joseph's son?'"

— LUKE 4:16-22

Jesus was demonstrating what God's House should look like, and the
ministry that should result from this vision. The pattern He established
was that we firstly worship God, and then we are anointed to reach people.

CLARITY OF MISSION RESULTS IN EQUIPPING PEOPLE

Our mission is to equip people for life through faith in Jesus Christ. In the
Equippers Network we see 'life' as being three-dimensional:

- Our faith in Christ affects the life we live now—our job, our
  relationships and marriages, our family, and our connection to
  church and the people in our world.

- Our faith in Christ helps prepare us for our life tomorrow. This
  is about stepping into God's vision for the future. This may be
  through educational training, growing in financial prosperity,
  or personal development.

- Our faith in Christ inspires us to steward our life in the light of
  eternity. Jesus set an example of living in view of what lies ahead.
  We read in Hebrews 12:2, "Looking unto Jesus, the author and
  finisher of our faith, who for the joy that was set before Him
  endured the cross, despising the shame, and has sat down at the
  right hand of the throne of God."

Our mission is very much aligned to the Great Commission given by Jesus Christ in Matthew 28:19-20:

> "Go therefore, and make disciples of all the nations, baptising them in the name of the Father and of the Son and of the Holy Spirit, teaching them to observe all things that I have commanded you; and lo, I am with you always, even to the end of the age."

CLARITY OF PURPOSE RESULTS IN GENERATIONAL UPTAKE

Mission fills our life with a sense of purpose, whereas values help us to understand what we are building. Ephesians 2:19-22 is an important scripture to help us develop Christ-centred values for His Church:

> "Now, therefore, you are no longer strangers and foreigners, but fellow citizens with the saints and members of the household of God, having been built on the foundation of the apostles and prophets, Jesus Christ Himself being the chief cornerstone, in whom the whole building, being fitted together, grows into a holy temple in the Lord, in whom you also are being built together for a dwelling place of God in the Spirit."

In simple terms, our beliefs are the foundations we build on. From my understanding we, as evangelical or pentecostal Christians, stand on a conservative foundation of beliefs. That's why we also need values. Values allow us to create a unique culture that can serve each church or movement to fulfil its particular mission. With Christ as the cornerstone we will not build haphazardly, but rather powerfully and with authority.

We serve the next generation by being clear about what we see. We do not serve them well by telling them what they should do. David knew

God had spoken, but he handed over the mandate to build God's house to his son. Godly vision should never be limited to one generation, but each generation has the freedom to fashion and fulfil the work that God has given through the brilliance of His grace. If we fail to create that freedom, we leave behind us institutions that are unbending and inflexible to the move of the Holy Spirit. Faith has the ability to see our future, while wisdom is needed to build what we see. Faith sees, wisdom builds!

8

Embrace Godly Values - I

All of us live with our personal preferences. Some are good and others, not so good. Sadly, for some people, their godly convictions and good preferences have changed over time in the name of 'progressive thinking'. We need to establish godly values because predetermined values create culture, and this is what people become aware of when they come into our environment. Some families enjoy their evening meal watching television with their dinner plate resting on their lap, while another family prefers to sit at a table with the television off so that everyone can interact. One, in my opinion, has a better result, but neither are inherently right or wrong. They are the outworking of preferences, and the end result is that culture is formed. As we have already seen, a positive way to establish our values or preferences is to have Jesus Christ and His Word as our Cornerstone.

Helen and I have sought to build our marriage on strong, clearly identifiable values. Our vision is constantly growing and evolving, but our values have enabled us to build a marriage that is strong and enduring. The year 2020, for us, marked fifty years of marriage, and what wonderful years they have been, doing life and having fun together. I honour Helen for her love, integrity, charm, beauty, generosity, strength, and for her amazing heart of service. She is not only a great wife, but also a fantastic mother and grandmother.

In the early years of our marriage, we were never taught about the importance of having godly values, but we did establish some preferences that we have built upon together. It's only as we have started teaching on marriage that we recognised these as values and saw that we now enjoy the blessings of the decisions we made earlier on.

Helen and I came from very similar backgrounds. Our parents had good marriages—in fact, Helen's parents went on to celebrate their seventieth wedding anniversary. By today's standards, we were married relatively young and we have never seen this as a disadvantage. In fact, I know of many strong, lasting marriages where the couples married young. One of the advantages is that you haven't developed strong, independent habits that need to be changed once married. I don't think it's necessary to put off the inevitable because a couple have limited finances, or are currently at university, or developing their career. These pressures can even serve to bring couples together and forge a closer relationship!

Helen and I grew up in the same town, went to the same schools, and held the same beliefs. The values we have built upon serve as the cornerstone of our marriage. They guide us as we journey through life together. For us, the following 'value statements' which we adopted have held us in good stead over the years:

LEAVE NOTHING UNDER THE CARPET

We have always been good at dealing with issues quickly, and we have no secrets. Things that are hidden can become the basis for problems that fester over time. Withholding, sulking, and bad moods are all forms of manipulation, just as being angry and overbearing can become forms of control. We understand that unforgiveness, offences, bitterness, and resentment can become a breeding ground for betrayal. With this in mind, we do not let the fear of being rejected rob us from being completely open about our weaknesses and walking in the light. 1 John 1:7 is a helpful verse:

> "But if we walk in the light as He is in the light, we have fellowship with one another, and the blood of Jesus Christ His Son cleanses us from all sin."

Once, Helen was cooking breakfast for a couple we were hosting in our home. Before leaving the kitchen for a brief moment, I watched as she flipped the first perfectly-browned pancake onto the plate. Upon my return, I saw a tower of twenty-five steaming pancakes on the plate! On its own, that one little pancake made very little impact, but twenty-five?! Now that was a sizeable stack!

At the time, we were helping a couple with a complex marriage problem, and God used this illustration to identify the importance of dealing with issues quickly. This couple had been sweeping their problems under the carpet. Now those problems had grown into what was now a very sizeable stack of issues and offences—a stack that, sadly, they could no longer deal with. When couples enter into an argument because someone 'forgot the milk' and it quickly escalates to the point of talking about divorce, it is a pretty clear sign of a pervading pancake-like stack of issues that haven't been dealt with!

On another occasion, someone informed me of an affair that they had never revealed to their spouse. My advice, for the sake of their future, was that they should share the secret. To my knowledge, that person never found the courage to tell their loved one, even though holding onto that secret would have left them bearing an enormous and unnecessary burden of guilt and shame. The Christian life must be characterised by living free from anything that weighs heavy upon us.

LOVE UNCONDITIONALLY

Love that holds us together can be best explained by three words: commitment, acceptance and forgiveness.

I am so thankful for Helen's unwavering commitment to me. Whenever I have opened the door of my soul and she has become aware of my humanity, she has accepted me and forgiven me. We hold to the traditional Christian vows: to love, to honour, and to cherish. Over the years we have identified certain attitudes in couples who are struggling in their marriage. When love breaks down, it is often because of anger, bitterness, unforgiveness, and control. These issues must be addressed or the relationship can become septic, oppressive, and dangerous, especially when the power becomes one-sided. Domestic violence is an ever-increasing concern in our society.

Helen and I decided that love, to us, means we will always seek to understand the other person's needs. Learning to accept one another is a powerful attribute of love. We defined 'honouring' as "valuing, respecting and placing one's weight behind the other," while 'cherishing' is looking after the other person's wellbeing, both practically and spiritually. We made a choice in the early stages of our marriage that our love for each other another would remain strong so that our children would grow in a loving environment where they would feel secure. We faced the fact that our children would one day leave us, and we built our lives together on the strong value of loving unconditionally and having a love that endures so that, even when our nest became empty, we would still enjoy and have one another.

Many couples separate at the point where their children are grown because all their love and attention has been fully directed towards the children, leaving their marriage love tank empty. A great verse to hold to in our relationships is 1 John 2:5: "But whoever keeps His word, truly the love of God is perfected in Him. By this we know that we are in Him."

WALK AS ONE

It's amazing how opposites attract and how the Holy Spirit can weld two opposites together as one. This is so true of Helen and I. Helen's spiritual gifts are mercy and serving, whereas mine are exhortation and prophecy. Even though we are different in our nature and motivations as male and female, and we often respond to situations very differently, we have sought to understand one another, knowing that God's desire is to build us together as a powerful team.

Discord in any relationship is an abomination to God, and lack of unity removes God's hand of blessing. That is why we must sit down and work on things we can agree and unite on together. Helen and I have found Amos 3:3 very helpful: "How can two walk together unless they agree?" We also read God's designed order for marriage in Genesis 2:24:

> "Therefore a man shall leave his father and mother and be
> joined to his wife, and they shall become one flesh."

God ordained marriage to be between a man and a woman, and He also stated they shall become as 'one flesh,' leaving their father and mother to establish their own identity. Marriage problems often exist when couples don't fully leave home, but continue to hold tightly to the influence of their parents.

Becoming one in heart and living in agreement is a decision we make, but each individual is responsible for the stewardship of their own gifts and relationship with God. Oneness can be easily damaged when a person starts to exchange that secret place reserved for marriage, becoming emotionally attached with someone other than their spouse. That is why the old saying is very true, "Those who pray together, stay together." Prayer is standing in agreement for a better future. It provides a secure anchor and sets up a marriage for longevity.

LIVE WITH ADVENTURE

It was the year 2000 when Helen and I moved to London to establish what is now Equippers Church there. We have found our adventures of faith to be a wonderful blessing, building our lives together and keeping us from becoming boring and predictable. Helen's parents demonstrated an adventure-filled life to us. In the early years of their retirement, they decided to buy a motorhome and took to the road for nine years. In fact, even in their early nineties, despite having a permanent home, they would still go travelling in their motorhome. Helen's dad didn't sell his last motorhome until he was ninety-six!

In New Zealand, the journey from the cradle to the grave can easily be mapped out, and we often find people bored in the middle stages of life because everything has become mundane and predictable. If this is not addressed, it can become a breeding ground for an array of unhealthy activities.

One day while living in London, we were taking our son Sam to Heathrow so he could catch his flight home when Helen said, "I feel disappointed that I am not in New Zealand for the grandchildren." Sam, in his wisdom, replied, "Mum, the greatest legacy you can leave my children is not being always there for them, but that you are still prepared to take risks of faith." Faith, in its very nature, is an adventure, and it keeps us in a healthy place of trusting God. A wonderful verse to hold onto as we live our faith-adventures is 1 John 5:4, "For whatever is born of God overcomes the world. And this is the victory that has overcome the world—our faith."

HAVE GODLY PURPOSE

Throughout our marriage, Helen and I have walked with godly purpose. We share the same passion for the house of God and a love for seeing the gospel of the kingdom of God established in people's lives. Even though our functions may be different, we hold the same purpose, and because of this we are able work together without friction in areas of giving and serving. In fact, I believe this is one of the reasons why all our children love the house of God. I have been inspired over the years as I have observed older people still loving Jesus, connected to church, serving people, and committed to godly purpose. This is what Psalm 92 means when it says:

"Those who are planted in the house of the Lord shall flourish in the courts of our God. They shall still bear fruit in old age; they shall be fresh and flourishing" (v. 13-14).

Another relevant verse is Philippians 3:14, "I press towards the goal for the prize of the upward call of God in Christ Jesus." This is especially pertinent to those who are mature in age, given that Paul wrote this at the later stage of his life. I cannot over-state the importance of strong values. From the beginning of our marriage, we established these important preferences because, together, we knew what we wanted our marriage to look like. The values we agreed upon kept our vision clear and gave us the blocks to build with.

Vision is constantly developing and is progressive, whereas values do not change and therefore produce the characteristics of a unique and defined culture. Values help couples establish principles that are not easily broken. Separation only becomes possible when couples haven't built well or are not prepared to walk together through the valley of conflict to craft a new future. This verse plants a powerful image in our minds of God's plan and purpose for marriage, assisting us to work toward a complete, wholehearted, and united relationship.

The same principle applies to us all—when we establish godly values, our lives become anchored, positioning us to leave a legacy that enables others to flourish.

9

Embrace Godly Values - II

We have seen that foundations are formed from our beliefs, while our values establish culture, and yet we find that people are more likely to join a church on the basis of the feel of the environment rather than the beliefs the church passionately upholds. It has been said that people visiting a church service decide very quickly whether or not they will return. This decision is usually based on their intuition. When I visit other churches, I am especially conscious of their welcome. I notice if the atmosphere is filled with hope, and whether there is a spirit of joy and thanksgiving. I ask myself if I feel edified through the ministry and whether I feel challenged to grow in my relationship with Christ.

Apostolic and prophetic ministers need to be diligent in establishing the foundations of belief in a church. Although they may go unseen on an initial visit, it is these Christ-centred biblical beliefs that create security and help direct people towards a life-giving relationship with Jesus. Though the foundations are rarely seen, the values of a church can be witnessed and felt from the get-go. They create the culture. When a visitor enters a church that has a spirit of excellence and a genuine heart to serve, that person will experience something special, whether as a result of their initial welcome, the music, the ministry, people's attitudes through giving, or, perhaps, the hosting of God's presence.

The values of the Equippers Network illustrate the importance of reproducing a Holy Spirit-inspired culture with Jesus Christ as our chief cornerstone. The 'cornerstone' was historically used by builders to ensure that a building was straight, or plumb, and on the level. Today, it's called a 'profile'.

We use the acronym H-E-A-R-T to identify our values, which we refer to as the 'five heartbeats of Equippers'.

1. THE HEARTBEAT OF HONOUR

One of our defining scriptures is found in Exodus 33:12-16, where we read a dialogue between God and Moses. In verse 14, God says to Moses, "My presence will go with you, and I will give you rest." Moses responds by saying, "If your presence does not go with us, do not bring us up from here" (v. 15).

God had promised Moses that He would bring the children of Israel to a 'land of milk and honey,' but on the way the people grieved the Spirit of God with their stubborn attitude. In Exodus 33:3 God says to them,

> "Go up to the land flowing with milk and honey; for I will not go
> up in your midst, lest I consume you on the way, for you are a
> stiff-necked people."

What God was saying was that even though they would still inhabit the land He had offered them, He wasn't going to journey with them because they had become stubborn and inflexible in their hearts.

We are committed to building a church that honours the presence of the Holy Spirit and its anointing. In the last chapter I shared that the word 'honour' means "to value, to respect, to put weight behind." Therefore, as a church, we seek to value the Holy Spirit's presence and place our weight behind what is on His agenda.

We honour His Word. Sadly, there are far too many biblically illiterate Christians in the church, people who flounder through life because they haven't taken time to study the Word of God. Paul instructed Timothy as a young man, "Be diligent to present yourself approved to God, a worker who does not need to be ashamed, rightly dividing the word of truth" (2 Timothy 2:15). The Word of God prepares us to live a life of integrity. It helps us to establish a sure foundation to build upon, and it becomes the inspiration for faith to grow. In Acts 2:42 we read how the early church devoted themselves to the apostles' teaching. From my observation, people who have established their lives upon the Word of God are not easily tossed around during a season of difficulty.

In addition to honouring the Holy Spirit and the Word of God, we honour the grace-gift of leadership. Leadership can be taught, but in the end it is the people with an 'X-factor' who make the greatest difference. They have a special grace on their lives to inspire vision, communicate direction, build people together in teams, and call people to action. One of Equippers' axioms is "Building together with leadership-led teams." We often use the analogy of sports teams to help illustrate the diversity of skills needed for each position, while highlighting the role of the captain (leader), and the coach.

2. THE HEARTBEAT OF EXCELLENCE

I love how Daniel encapsulates the value of excellence.

> "Then this Daniel distinguished himself above the governors and satraps, because an excellent spirit was in him; and the king gave thought to setting him over the whole realm."
>
> — DANIEL 6:3

When we teach about excellence at Equippers, we address it as the overflow of a person's life. It is doing the best with what we have and living a blessed and prosperous life while upholding God's kingdom and the work He has assigned to us as our utmost priority. We believe excellence positions the church as 'a light on a hill' for all to see, revealing the vibrant colours of God's kingdom. Let's not give God our leftovers. Let's give Him our best as we seek His kingdom first!

The message of the book of Malachi in the Old Testament is firstly a message of correction. The people of God had resorted to bringing offerings that were marred, scarred, and second-rate. It was almost as if God was saying, "I am not interested in your leftovers."

Our God is an extravagant God—a God of abundance who loves to lavish His grace upon us. He gives us His best even when we don't deserve it. Romans 5:8 states, "But God demonstrates His own love toward us, in that while we were still sinners, Christ died for us." Here, we see the fullness of God's extravagant love demonstrated through the sacrificial death of Jesus Christ, upon the cross.

God also desires our 'first fruits'. Proverbs 3:9-10 says,

"Honour the Lord with your possessions, and with the first fruits of all your increase; so your barns will be filled with plenty, and your vats will overflow with new wine."

This scripture can refer to our attitude and efforts towards serving and our ministry to see the kingdom of God advance. However, this analogy also paints a picture that enables us to grasp an important practice and biblical principle: we bring our tithes and offerings to God. We can demonstrate an attitude of excellence by setting the first fruits of our income aside for our tithe instead of giving God our decomposing scraps—the rotten fruit at the bottom of the barrel that we no longer have use for.

I was not taught the blessing of bringing my tithes into the church. It was while reading Malachi 3:10 that the Holy Spirit spoke to me one day. That verse says,

> "'Bring all the tithes into the storehouse, that there may be food
> in My house, and try Me now in this,' says the Lord of hosts, 'if
> I will not open for you the windows of heaven and pour out for
> you such blessing that there will not be room enough to receive it.'"

From that day forward, I have never ceased to bring the first fruits of my income to God. Even when we have had moments of pressure with our finances, I hold to the truth that God deserves our best.

God also deserves our best when it comes to presentation. We must do everything we can to show off His splendour! This applies to how we present our facilities, music, ministry programmes, promotional material—every facet of our organisation and our Sunday services should demonstrate this spirit of excellence and boast of the God who placed that spirit within us. Matthew 5:14-16 (MSG) says,

> "Here's another way to put it: You're here to be light, bringing
> out the God-colours in the world. God is not a secret to be kept.
> We're going public with this, as public as a city on a hill. If I
> make you light-bearers, you don't think I'm going to hide you
> under a bucket, do you? I'm putting you on a light stand. Now
> that I've put you there on a hilltop, on a light stand—shine!
> Keep open house; be generous with your lives. By opening up to
> others, you'll prompt people to open up with God, this generous
> Father in heaven."

God's people and the church must not carry a spirit of excellence in theory alone—that excellence must be outworked and made visible so that others are drawn in. This was David's desire when he wrote, "Oh, magnify the Lord with me, and let us exalt His name together" (Psalm 34:3). God loves it when we boldly boast in His goodness and testify to the Holy Spirit's power.

3. THE HEARTBEAT OF ADVANCEMENT

Paul closed his second letter to the Corinthians with the words, "Finally brethren, farewell. Become complete . . ." (2 Corinthians 13:11). This word 'complete' is the same word in the Greek that is used in Matthew 4:21 for 'mending', in Ephesians 4:12 for 'equipping', and in Galatians 6:1, 'to restore'. Therefore, at Equippers we teach that we must be advancing in all areas of our life. The salvation of Jesus Christ is not just a decision, but a journey. Our goal must be to become more like Him. We teach that we must advance:

In leading ourselves. At the very heart of the gospel of Jesus Christ is not only God's plan for humanity, but also the power to help every person to take personal responsibility for their own destiny. Our mission at Equippers is to do all we can to "equip people for life through faith in Jesus Christ." This involves teaching people to lead themselves, to address character issues, to embrace accountability, to know their God-given gifts and discover how they are all individually wired, to develop in the adventure of faith, to find freedom, and how to endure. Excellent scriptures that increase our understanding in these areas include *Psalm 139:13-14; Romans 12:6-8; 1 Corinthians 12; Romans 5:3-5; and 2 Timothy 3:16-17.*

In leading others. Every one of us leads someone at a certain level. We all have influence over another life. This happens at home with our family, at work, in church, in the community and, for some, in a nation, or even internationally. Jesus taught that at the heart of every Christian leader should be servanthood (Luke 22:24-27, John 13:1-17). Servant leaders work for the benefit of others; they long to see everyone prosper. A servant-hearted person comes under people rather than assuming a position over those entrusted to their care. Insecure people try to 'lord it' over others because they don't want to be personally accountable. When a church takes on the heart of servanthood, however, it is very attractive and a wonderful environment to be in. Servant-heartedness has become the foundation of our ministries, and we take pleasure in equipping and empowering people.

In leading our world. Innovation, creativity, adventure, and taking ground are all strong biblical themes. We believe Christians must become leaders in their worlds—in education, the arts, business, and science. As well as taking God into our worlds, we should unashamedly seek to advance the kingdom of God, to bring light to a world that is tormented by confusion and insecurity. As Proverbs 4:18 says, ". . . the path of the just is like the shining sun, that shines ever brighter unto the perfect day."

4. THE HEARTBEAT OF REACHING OUT

I have mentioned that Equippers churches are churches 'on mission,' rather than having a 'missions department'. We believe we are called to reach out in order to take back territory from the enemy. The heartbeat of 'reaching out' is central to everything we do. It is our motivation for taking the gospel to the world by teaching every individual to be a soul-winner, planting Christ-centred churches, being involved in social action, extending God's heart of justice, empowering every Christian to minister in the power of God, and encouraging people to engage in acts of kindness. We believe the church of Jesus Christ exists to extend the kingdom of God, and not just focus on its own needs. We exist to equip people to impact their world! Key scriptures that speak to this include: *Mark 16:14-18; Matthew 4:23; Acts 10:38; James 2; and Matthew 5:13-16.*

5. THE HEARTBEAT OF TOGETHERNESS

Togetherness creates community. We cannot achieve God's purpose for our life in isolation. God designed His church to enable us to do and achieve so much more together than we ever could on our own. This is why at Equippers, we emphasise the importance of eGroups (or connect groups), leadership-led teams, common interest groups and ministry function groups. We also seek to build a sense of community through all our church activities. The heartbeat of 'being together, together' creates unity, family and friendships. Like any family, we need to guard against discord, division, or offences that create separation. Therefore, nothing goes under the carpet! We seek to walk in the light and maintain integrity in our relationships. The following verses highlight this heartbeat: *1 John 1:7; Psalm 133; Amos 3:3; and Ephesians 4:11-16.*

Most evangelical churches share the same 90% of foundational beliefs. This is healthy and good—it gives us a point of global connection and unity. It is my belief, however, that churches should have different expressions, and that these are derived from the values we hold. It is disappointing to see many significant ministries and organisations fail to survive beyond their founders. This happens when they are established around the charisma of one person or emphasis, rather than being built upon enduring values. When our unique values are established with Jesus Christ as the chief cornerstone, they become a lot easier to pass on from generation to generation. This allows us to build with longevity in mind.

PART FOUR

GROWTH AND MATURITY

10

Embrace the Flow - I

The Holy Spirit wants to strengthen every Christian from the inside out. We can identify this burden in the Apostle Paul's prayer for the church in Ephesians 3:14-21 (ESV, emphasis mine):

> "For this reason I bow my knees before the Father, from whom every family in heaven and on earth is named, that according to the riches of his glory **he may grant you to be strengthened with power through his Spirit in your inner being, so that Christ may dwell in your hearts through faith**—that you, being rooted and grounded in love, may have strength to comprehend with all the saints what is the breadth and length and height and depth, and to know the love of Christ that surpasses knowledge, that you may be filled with all the fullness of God. **Now to him who is able to do far more abundantly than all that we ask or think, according to the power at work within us,** to him be glory in the church and in Christ Jesus throughout all generations, forever and ever. Amen."

The 'far more abundantly than all that we ask or think,' comes from the power that works within us. The following three scriptures carry the same thought:

"... he who is in you is greater than he who is in the world."

— 1 John 4:4

"To them God willed to make known what are the riches of the glory of this mystery among the Gentiles: which is Christ in you, the hope of glory."

— Colossians 1:27

"On the last day of the feast, the great day, Jesus stood up and cried out, 'If anyone thirsts, let him come to me and drink. Whoever believes in me, as the Scripture has said, "Out of his heart will flow rivers of living water."' Now this he said about the Spirit, whom those who believed in him were to receive, for as yet the Spirit had not been given, because Jesus was not yet glorified."

— John 7:37-39 (ESV)

From this scripture in John's gospel, Jesus identifies five areas that develop the flow of life: thirsts (inner desire), beliefs (in Himself, Jesus Christ), heart (out of the heart), flow, and living (from the inside out).

The prophet Ezekiel uses similar prophetic imagery to describe a vision he received. Ezekiel's name means, "God strengthens." Through Ezekiel, God's desire was to build strength back into the nation of Israel. Ezekiel used prophecies, parables, signs and symbols to convey God's message to an exiled people. In Ezekiel 37 they are described as being like dry bones in the sun, an army that God would reassemble and breathe life into. This is a prophecy about Israel's restoration, but it also serves as a picture of the Church and of our own lives.

In Ezekiel 47 the prophet uses a different picture to speak of accessing the anointing of God, and the subsequent power that would ultimately impact nations:

"Then he brought me back to the door of the temple, and behold, water was issuing from below the threshold of the temple toward the east (for the temple faced east). The water was flowing down from below the south end of the threshold of the temple, south of the altar. Then he brought me out by way of the north gate and led me around on the outside to the outer gate that faces toward the east; and behold, the water was trickling out on the south side.

Going on eastward with a measuring line in his hand, the man measured a thousand cubits, and then led me through the water, and it was ankle-deep. Again he measured a thousand, and led me through the water, and it was knee-deep. Again he measured a thousand, and led me through the water, and it was waist-deep. Again he measured a thousand, and it was a river that I could not pass through, for the water had risen. It was deep enough to swim in, a river that could not be passed through. And he said to me, 'Son of man, have you seen this?'

Then he led me back to the bank of the river. As I went back, I saw on the bank of the river very many trees on the one side and on the other. And he said to me, 'This water flows toward the eastern region and goes down into the Arabah, and enters the sea; when the water flows into the sea, the water will become fresh. And wherever the river goes, every living creature that swarms will live, and there will be very many fish. For this water goes there, that the waters of the sea may become fresh; so everything will live where the river goes. Fishermen will stand beside the sea. From Engedi to Eneglaim it will be a place for the spreading of nets. Its fish will be of very many kinds, like the fish of the Great Sea. But its swamps and marshes will not become fresh; they are to be left for salt. And on the banks, on both sides of the river, there will grow all kinds of trees for food. Their leaves will not wither, nor their fruit fail, but they will bear fresh fruit every month, because the water for them flows from the sanctuary. Their fruit will be for food, and their leaves for healing.'"

— Ezekial 47:1-2 (ESV)

One of the axioms of Equippers is, "a river without banks becomes a swamp." This is so true in life. We need good boundaries that can control the flow of our lives, enabling it to increase and have a lasting impact. Many people set out with good intentions but because they don't take time to build these vital boundaries—or riverbanks—in their lives, much of what they do ends up taking on the characteristics of a swamp. The water becomes stagnant and putrid, like a breeding ground for mosquitoes. Many problems in life can be traced back to careless decisions, simply because people did not predetermine the vision and values that would serve as their banks. Defined boundaries enable us to contain the flow released by the Holy Spirit—a flow which positively impacts all it touches, bringing healing to our environment and an abundance of fruit wherever the river flows.

From this vision of the river in Ezekiel we glean insight into five important phases that can help us build an ever-increasing flow of blessing and momentum that will impact our own lives as well as the church.

1. THE DECISION PHASE

In Ezekiel, the water originates at the temple before flowing out through the south side of the temple. This imagery depicts the decision phase in the life of a Christian. It is the beginning of our journey, the moment when we become a fully surrendered follower of Jesus Christ.

When I gave my life to Christ at the age of twelve, my commitment was valid. Something happened within me, but with a lack of good discipleship, my teenage years were lived without healthy boundaries and were marred by bad choices. The young farmers in our location were known to be hard workers but we also partied hard. As I have already shared, this changed soon after my car accident.

Helen, on the other hand, had been actively involved in Christian groups throughout her teenage years and has many fond memories of genuine godly encounters that resulted through positive leadership and good discipleship. Not long after we were married, one of her leaders, Peter Yarrell, along with his wife Jilly, took us sailing for a couple of days in the Marlborough Sounds at the top of the South Island in New Zealand.

New Zealand is one of the places on earth where God truly shows off His creative ability! The Marlborough Sounds are awe-inspiring, with native forests clothing the hills right down to the water's edge. The sound of the bird life never ceases to catch your attention. On our holiday together, we sailed from one bay to another, stopping at times to fish and to visit quaint restaurants tucked away from the fast pace of life. But Peter's ultimate plan was to talk about our faith, and we became a captive audience.

When we returned home, Helen and I decided to visit our local Anglican Church where approximately fifteen people regularly gathered for worship. The church had just appointed a new vicar, and for the first time in many years, I heard the gospel preached. After the service we returned to our farmhouse, where we both made a commitment to be 'all out for God' and by His grace we have remained steadfast to that decision. This became the foundation of just about every major decision we would make from that point forward. Like the temple vision Ezekiel had, this was the awakening of God's Spirit in our lives.

The same analogy is found in Proverbs 4:23: "Keep your heart with all diligence, for *out of it springs the issues of life.*" And in John's gospel the same thought is spoken by Jesus:

> "On the last day, that great day of the feast, Jesus stood and cried out, saying, 'If anyone thirsts, let him come to Me and drink. He who believes in Me, as the Scripture has said, *out of his heart will flow rivers of living water.*' But this He spoke concerning the Spirit, whom those believing in Him would receive; for the Holy Spirit was not yet given, because Jesus was not yet glorified."
> — JOHN 7:37-39 (EMPHASIS MINE)

Paul then adds a generational component to the picture where he says:

> "Now to Him who is able to do exceedingly abundantly above all that we ask or think, according to the power that works in us, to Him be glory in the church by Christ Jesus to all generations, forever and ever. Amen."
> — EPHESIANS 3:20-21

Every great move of God throughout history has begun in the human heart. William Booth, the founder of the Salvation Army said, "The greatness of a man's power is in the measure of his surrender." Revival begins *in a heart that is completely surrendered* to the will and purposes of God. When we surrender, strength increases and divine conviction grows. In the words of C.S. Lewis, "The more we let God take us over, the more truly ourselves we become."

Surrender can be best demonstrated through our obedience and trust, which sets us free from a self-imposed prison of fear. The words of Paul in Philippians 3:7 capture this thought when he says, "But what things were gain to me I have counted loss for Christ." Paul's life testifies to the fact that these were not just mere words. He allowed his love and surrender to Jesus Christ to keep him centred.

In Acts 20:24, when warning about impending tribulation, Paul tells the elders of the church at Ephesus, "But none of these things move me; nor do I count my life dear to myself, so that I may finish my race with joy, and the ministry which I received from the Lord Jesus, to testify to the gospel of the grace of God." Because he was centred, he remained focused.

It is easy to preach from passages like this, but it is another thing to live them out. Every time the Holy Spirit leads me down a new path or takes me to another level, He requires a new position of surrender. When we surrender, we lay down rights, give away personal and political agendas, and take hold of God's divine mandate.

The picture I take from this first phase of the vision in Ezekiel 47 is one of a vessel surrendered before God, anointed by the Holy Spirit and ready to allow God-inspired initiatives to be born. There is clear vision for the future, but it is yet to be unravelled, and a conviction of kingdom purpose is yet to be determined. As a believer comes to that place of surrender, they willingly start to take their first steps of obedience. This is when the Holy Spirit's anointing starts to flow from the vessel. It does not begin with a flood, but it does begin to flow. At this phase everything seems concealed from others, but it begins to consume the carrier as though nothing else matters.

Many years ago I wrote in the front of my Bible that my Holy Spirit-inspired mission and vision in life was to "equip and empower another generation," and "to establish apostolic houses of influence in major cities around the world." These goals have consumed my life, and I am very intentional about how I live. I do all I can to serve these God-given dreams. I don't want to finish my time on this earth wondering about (or limiting) His plan. Like the Apostle Paul, I want to be able to say, "I have fought the good fight, I have finished the race, I have kept the faith" (2 Timothy 4:7). But it all begins with a moment of decision and surrender.

11

Embrace the Flow - II

As we continue to look at Ezekiel's vision, we see the importance of each subsequent phase as God's anointing flows from the temple and begins to gain momentum. It is my prayer that as I share this revelation our sense of our need for the Holy Spirit would increase and that we would take seriously the words of Joshua in Joshua 3:5: "Sanctify yourselves, for tomorrow the Lord will do wonders among you."

Let's continue looking at how we can develop a life that is abundantly blessed so that we can become people who bless others.

2. THE PREPARATION PHASE (Ankle deep)

The account in Ezekiel 47 details how the water flowed from the temple. From there, Ezekiel was instructed to measure one thousand cubits (about 533 metres) downstream, and then to cross over. By that stage, the stream had accumulated enough water that it reached Ezekiel's ankles. One of the interesting features of a river is that the greater the flow of water, the stronger the banks need to be. We've already seen that a river without banks will inevitably become a mere swamp—a breeding ground for all kinds of horrible creatures.

The decisions we make in this phase of our Christian lives are very important. We need to be intentional about building banks for the ministry that God wants to produce in and through our lives. That ministry or vision could be the establishment of a church, a ministry within a church or movement of churches, a kingdom business, a successful marriage, or the raising of children. If we prepare well, the ultimate impact of what God is releasing through our lives will be greater.

We can establish our banks during this phase by:

- Confirming what we believe. Our beliefs will become the foundation of everything we do. I would say I am conservative in my belief, but contemporary in my expression.

- Building into our lives the discipline of prayer, bible reading, journal writing, mediation and devotion. We are never too busy to pray. I have observed how prayer can become really important when we are in a crisis or need. I have determined, however, to build all of my life around prayer and devotion, and to increase the depth of my prayer deposits before God's throne.

- Establishing the values we are going to build with. These values determine how we operate. Good values then become our plumb line when we face conflicting voices or a crisis.

- Making a commitment to be generous. It is essential to cement a spirit of generosity as a cornerstone in our lives. Helen and I have practiced the discipline of tithing and giving for over fifty years simply because we made this value-based decision at the beginning of our marriage.

- Planting ourselves in a local church and becoming active members. Christians are not saved to live in isolation but to become active members of the body of Christ. The older I become, the more I enjoy the outworking of Psalm 92:13-15: "Those who are planted in the house of the Lord shall flourish in the courts of our God. They shall still bear fruit in old age; they shall be fresh and flourishing, to declare that the Lord is upright; He is my rock, and there is no unrighteousness in Him."

- Committing to keeping our faith levels high, because there will be times of discouragement.

- Choosing to fill our lives with kingdom purpose and the cause of Christ. When we make this our priority, our lives are never stagnant—they are filled with adventure. As a young man I could never have predicted the life I now live, or the overflowing joy Christ brings by making His kingdom purposes my priority.

- Determining to lead like Christ. Servant leadership is contagious, and constantly works for the benefit of others.

With our banks in place, we can then begin to model the vision that we see. Proverbs 14:18 (MSG) says, "Foolish dreamers live in a world of illusion; wise realists plant their feet on the ground." When I first secured my farm as a young man, I was able to obtain a scaled aerial photo of the property. For weeks I planned, from my lounge, how I wanted my farm to look. This exercise proved to be invaluable and taught me the importance of the preparation phase.

It was at this time that I also learned four important lessons from Habakkuk 2:1-4:

1. The importance of prayer and waiting on God. *"I will stand on my watch" (v. 1).*

2. The importance of writing down what you see. *"Write the vision and make it plain on tablets that he may run who reads it" (v. 2).*

3. The importance of preparation and seasons. *"For the vision is yet for an appointed time; but at the end it will speak, and it will not lie. Though it tarries, wait for it; because it will surely come, it will not tarry" (v. 3).*

4. The importance of living with a strong conviction of faith. *"But the just shall live by faith" (v. 4).*

When we spend due time and diligence on the preparation stage, our efforts will be rewarded. By prayerfully working through our values and the decisions they require, we can be sure of a massive dividend in the long run.

3. THE EMPOWERMENT PHASE (knee deep)

In the next phase, Ezekiel was encouraged to walk yet another 533 metres before crossing the river again. This time, the level of the water reached his knees. The preparation phase had paid off, and the level of anointing and influence increased. At every phase, the key requirement is to strengthen our banks so they can contain the increased volume of what God is doing. Otherwise, we run the risk of losing what has been gained.

Every great river has tributaries that feed into it and add to its volume. This is also true of us when we are developing in areas of ministry, leadership, and church or organisational growth. Jesus understood the dilemma. He said to His disciples:

> "The harvest is plentiful, but the labourers are few. Therefore pray
> to the Lord of the harvest to send out labourers into His harvest."
> — MATTHEW 9:37-38

In simple terms, we need help. We need wisdom to build with people who will complement and serve the vision that God has entrusted to us from the beginning. If the preparation phase has been worked through properly, the people who are added to the team will serve the vision and work within the values that have been established. To help ensure that this happens, we will need to familiarise these people with our vision and values, making sure they've fully understood and grasped them. As I mentioned earlier, this is why we developed the 'five heartbeats of Equippers'. The visionary leader is responsible for ensuring people are well informed of the values that will carry their vision and enable it to succeed. It is interesting to watch the conversation change as people embrace values and vision. One of the initial changes that takes place is a shift in language from words like 'me and mine' to 'us and ours'.

If we are to increase the flow or volume in our lives, we must learn the importance of delegating responsibility. When delegating a task, we need to be careful to define the start and the endpoint. While others may take responsibility for a task, it is my responsibility to ensure that everything is implemented in the manner I have perceived, and that it reinforces our values and culture. I take note of the person's response to time management, along with their follow-through, teachability, attitude, and the way they work with others. I am also observing their response to, and respect of, my leadership.

Organisations grow when we empower people. An empowered leader takes full responsibility for their department, while the senior leader's major role is to protect and strengthen the banks, because they become a carrier of the vision, along with the visionary leader. This is crucial if influence is to increase. In my observation, the reason many organisations and churches cannot work through this phase is because their senior leaders will not empower others and feel the need to always be in control.

At this point in the river, the volume of water against Ezekiel's knees was strong enough to make him feel insecure, but he could still hold on. To go to yet another phase, he would eventually need to 'let go'. Whenever we empower people, we are letting go. We are less concerned about their approach than about productivity and fruitfulness. We are looking for results, so the person will need to have a 'whatever it takes' attitude.

I cannot overemphasise the importance of empowerment if we are to see the Church increase in influence. And as we empower others, it is important that we pay attention to our own character growth, understanding of people's unique gifting, and development of our skills. We must develop a deeper trust in God's faithfulness even when things don't work out the way we originally thought they would, knowing that pressure builds strength.

4. THE INCREASE PHASE (waist deep)

A further 533 metres along, Ezekiel found himself waist-deep as he crossed the river. With the increased depth, it was now difficult for him to hold his footing. It is at this stage, for us, that we need to be very discerning. As the flow and capacity in our lives increase, the devil will attempt to divert us from God's original purpose. We need to remain in a place of humility and dependence on the Holy Spirit.

This is a season when everything is tested. As a result there will often be tension, and 'stretch-marks' may appear as people's motivations are revealed. God allows His people to be tested at every stage of life, but during this phase, the enemy will do all he can to override the purposes of God. His intention is to distract God's people because he realises that the power and influence of their life is about to increase exponentially. Many organisations and significant anointed ministries have failed at this stage as they faced the following tests:

The Test of Humility

At this stage, success is increasing and influence is spreading. As a result, people start to take notice of what is happening. The danger zone (or the human 'minefield') that is often hidden from view is in the area of our internal reactions. It is easy to start thinking of ourselves as being more important or powerful than we actually are. In saying this, I am not devaluing the significance of our obedience, the development of our gifts, the influence of God's grace, or the impact of the Holy Spirit's anointing upon our life. But God does resist the proud and give grace to the humble.

"But He gives more grace. Therefore He says; God resists the proud, but gives more grace to the humble. Therefore submit to God. Resist the devil and he will flee from you."

— JAMES 4:6-7

The Test of Community

In Acts 20:28-31, Paul appealed to the elders of the church at Ephesus to always be on guard and to protect the church:

> "Therefore take heed to yourselves and to all the flock, among which the Holy Spirit has made you overseers, to shepherd the church of God which He purchased with His own blood. For I know this, that after my departure savage wolves will come in among you, not sparing the flock. Also from among yourselves men will rise up, speaking perverse things, to draw away the disciple after themselves. Therefore watch, and remember that for three years I did not cease to warn everyone day and night with tears."

The church of Jesus Christ is ripped apart every time a leader elevates their own gift and ministry, or draws people to themselves rather than to the Lord Jesus Christ. We all need to disciple others, but we must do so with a 'John the Baptist model' in mind— "He must increase, but I must decrease" (John 3:30). The test of community is about striving to protect the unity of the Spirit.

The Test of Commitment

The true test of commitment comes when pressure is applied. That's when we find what is really in the heart of a leader. Jesus is still the greatest discerner of people's hearts. In John 2:23-25 we read,

> "... many believed in His name when they saw the signs which He did. But Jesus did not commit Himself to them, because He knew all men, and had no need that anyone should testify of man, for *He knew what was in man*."

Every time God challenges His people with a new vision or direction, it will require them to increase their commitment. Many churches and organisations struggle at this point because the leadership are not brave enough to face the challenges involved. I find that my motivation actually grows at this point when I think of all the people who will be added to the kingdom! We must not let any negative voices derail what Jesus is calling us to do.

The Test of Time

As a young man, someone said to me, "If you want something done, ask a busy person." It sounds like a contradiction but, in reality, busy people know how to budget their time and focus it with intent. Every one of us has the same amount of time, and good leaders are not afraid to ask people for more time. But if we are going to move to the next level, it is paramount that we maximise the time allotted to us and work within our gifts and abilities. One of my mottos is, "live life with purpose and enjoy the journey."

The Test of Resources

As we experience increase there will be challenges on many fronts. This includes our resources. To grow, we will require more money, bigger buildings, more people, and greater expertise. This is when our faith is tested to the max. I am inspired by the testimony of George Muller who, in the 1800s, established the Ashley Down Orphanage in Bristol, England. This ministry, which ultimately grew to accommodate 2,500 children, was completely sustained through prayer and by faith. When someone remarked, "you must have a great gift of faith," George Mueller's reply was, "No, just a seed faith that has grown year by year."

We should never say we have arrived in our journey of faith, but allow ourselves to continually be challenged as we trust God for the resources we need to build to the next level.

The Test of Focus

The temptation to turn aside or give up simply because we cannot be bothered facing 'another round' is destructive both in ministry and in life. Many significant church leaders are now selling real estate or insurance, having moved in a completely new direction. Often this started with the thought that they just needed some time out. This sounds okay, but one year can easily become two, and before long, it seems impossible for them to refocus on the calling they once felt so strongly God had called them to do. The powerful sermons they once preached no longer move their own hearts.

God wants us to persevere and succeed because it glorifies Him. He is committed to our prosperity because it demonstrates His goodness. He wants to increase the sphere of our influence because it extends His kingdom. He wants to empower us with His grace because it moves us from the natural to the supernatural, and He wants us to maintain an attitude of humility towards Him so He can heal our land. In the face of increase, my prayer is, "Please, Jesus, help me to stay focused."

5. THE IMPACT PHASE (fully immersed)

When Ezekiel goes a further 533 metres deeper, his feet cannot touch the bottom. Now he is immersed in a river that no one can walk across, but can only swim in. In this phase, momentum has increased to such a level that it is completely beyond human control. Again, the responsibility of leadership is to ensure that the banks are strong enough to direct the flow and the work of the Holy Spirit. In this phase, growth becomes exponential. There is a level of corporate anointing that can only be described as, "exceedingly abundantly above all that we could ask or think" (Ephesians 3:20).

Leaders cannot simply kick back and relax in this stage. In fact, they must be even more diligent in making sure the values and vision stay on course. A large river's banks can still break, and because of the force of the water, it has the potential to carve a new course, one which probably is not in line with the original vision.

In an article written by VN Mukundarajan titled, "Life lessons from the Choluteca Bridge," he tells of a bridge built over the Choluteca River in Honduras. This small Central American nation is known for its horrific hurricanes, and the bridge needed to be able to withstand extreme forces of nature. The government initiated the project, recruiting a Japanese firm to build a bridge to connect with a new bypass road, using the latest and greatest technology at the time.

The construction of the bridge lasted two years and was completed in 1998. Just a few months after the bridge was opened, Hurricane Mitch struck, depositing seventy-five inches of rain in four days. That's equivalent to what the region would usually receive in six months! The river flooded and devastatingly, more than seven thousand people lost their lives. The hurricane wiped out all of the bridges along the river, sparing just one—the Choluceta bridge. The technology had withstood the brunt of this severe storm! Yet soon, another problem arose. Although the bridge did not crumble in the storm, the river that had once flowed beneath it had broken its banks and changed course as a result of the hurricane. Instead of flowing beneath the bridge, the river now flowed beside it. In the words of Mukundarajan, "The Choluteca bridge became a bridge to nowhere."

In Ezekiel's vision, it was only as the river stayed on course that it could it fulfil God's original purpose. Wherever it flowed it brought healing. Fish bred in abundance, and all kinds of trees flourished on its banks, producing fruit to eat and leaves for medicine.

The book of Acts gives us a picture of this phase as the early church multiplied, significantly impacting the world. Multiplication is very much on the heart of God because as the kingdom of God is extended and more people are equipped to fulfil God's purpose, churches become salt and light to their communities. Sadly, the church in many places around the world has lost its voice and no longer serves or preserves the community. It would appear, in many places, that the banks have broken, and institutionalism and tradition are now in control. Matthew 5:13 reads:

> "You are the salt of the earth; but if the salt loses its flavour, how shall it be seasoned? It is then good for nothing but to be thrown out and trampled underfoot by men."

This verse alludes to Ezekiel 47:11 which says:

> "But its swamps and marshes will not be healed; they will be given over to salt."

Both of these verses demonstrate the danger of stagnation. This occurs when we begin serving only to keep the wheels spinning, without any regard to forward progress. The constant danger of any organisation as it reaches the impact phase is institutionalism. Policy and rules stifle fresh initiatives, sucking the life out of the organisation. Positive momentum becomes a leader's best friend simply because it makes the leader look far better than they really are, but it is also a place where fresh levels of surrender are required. If this describes the phase you are in, you might like to pray this prayer:

Heavenly Father, today I surrender my life to You afresh and declare that it is my delight to do Your will. I humble myself before You, Jesus. I receive Your enabling grace and, by faith, open myself to a fresh impartation of Your anointing, Holy Spirit. I ask that the eyes of my heart would be enlightened to the hope of Your call and that You would give me the ability to see all that You are calling me to do. Help me, Jesus, to be defined by Your love so that I am secure enough to be fully immersed in Your purpose: to see Your kingdom established here on earth as it is in heaven. I pray this in Your name, Jesus Christ, my Lord. Amen!

12

Embrace Maturity

Having been involved in ministry for over forty years, one of my great joys is witnessing what I often refer to as 'redemption lift'. This is when people, having been released from places of brokenness and oppression, step into freedom, purpose, and fruitfulness. They leave the reign and dominion of sin and bondage, and enter into the region of grace, mercy, and truth. In this place, freedom reigns.

THE IMPORTANCE OF THE LOCAL CHURCH

Traditionally, the early church came together every Sunday to celebrate the resurrection of Jesus Christ, and throughout the centuries this tradition has been maintained.

In Equippers churches, members are encouraged to attend weekly corporate celebrations where they engage in songs of thanksgiving and praise, acknowledge the presence of the Holy Spirit, and receive anointed ministry from people who operate in the gifts of grace which God has given to the church to help every member grow in their faith. This is clearly detailed in Ephesians where Paul, the great Christian leader, points to a pathway that, when followed, will enable believers to mature.

In Ephesians 4:11-16 we read:

> "And He Himself gave some to be apostles, some prophets, some
> evangelists, and some pastors and teachers, for the equipping of
> the saints for the work of ministry, for the edifying of the body
> of Christ, till we all come to the unity of the faith and of the
> knowledge of the Son of God, to a perfect man, to the measure
> of the stature of the fullness of Christ; that we should no longer
> be children, tossed to and fro and carried about with every wind
> of doctrine, by the trickery of men, in the cunning craftiness of
> deceitful plotting, but, speaking the truth in love, may grow up
> in all things into Him who is the head—Christ—from whom
> the whole body, joined and knit together by what every joint
> supplies, according to the effective working by which every part
> does its share, causes growth of the body for the edifying of
> itself in love."

I have observed throughout my years of ministry, that people who build
into their lives the discipline of being connected to a local church family
develop an enduring faith that is able to hold them through the rough patches
of life and strongly equip them for what they are called to do.

Throughout the week, members of Equippers are encouraged to be
part of an eGroup (small group), where they can enjoy fellowship, build
lifelong friendships, find support through prayer and understanding and
grow through the study of God's Word. Because we see the church as one
large extended family, we also encourage people to carry responsibility for
the house by serving in some capacity on Sunday. Many of our churches
use hired venues, packing in early on Sunday mornings and packing out
at the end of the day. This is a labour intensive job that requires an army
of committed volunteers.

These are the internal functions of the church, made up by people, but the ultimate purpose is to equip individuals for the ministry God has called us to—expanding the kingdom of Christ on earth as it is in heaven.

GOD'S PROCESS OF CHANGE

We can only embark on God's pathway to maturity when we understand and embrace His process of change. The consequence of the fall of Adam and Eve was that a destructive virus called sin started to work against the glory of God's creation. Before the fall, both Adam and Eve knew what it was to live without sin, shame, fear, and oppression. They ruled and reigned with God, enjoying an untarnished relationship with Him and functioning under His creative order. Life was never boring as they worked closely with God in the garden of His creation. Their personal identities were secure because of the Father's unfailing love, and they enjoyed the freedom of functioning in God's gifts of grace. Their lives were blessed, and they prospered in everything they did.

When Adam and Eve ate from the tree of the knowledge of good and evil, they opened a door for sin to enter their lives, robbing them of God's glory and eroding God's perfect intention for them. From that day, the enemy found an entry point to cut across God's creative order. But Jesus, through His death on the cross and resurrection, enables us to be restored.

On my computer I have a virus scanner called 'CleanMe'. My computer was designed to function perfectly, but because it is exposed to external forces (including myself!), I need to regularly run the scanner to make sure it hasn't been maligned, and I also need to clean the rubbish bin. God's loving plan of redemption put in place His plan to restore you and I back to His creative intention for our lives. Jesus is my 'CleanMe'!

The root meaning of the word 'sin' is to 'miss the mark'. Whenever I sin, I am being directed away from God's best, making room for destructive forces to work against me. When we open our hearts to Christ, we give the Holy Spirit the right to begin this process of transformation and change. This happens through our confession of need, accepting His loving forgiveness, the renewal of our mind, and receiving a new vision to live a blessed life. I have found 2 Corinthians 3:17-18 helpful in understanding this process:

> "Now the Lord is the Spirit; and where the Spirit of the Lord is, there is liberty. But we all, with unveiled face, beholding as in a mirror the glory of the Lord, are being transformed into the same image from glory to glory, just as by the Spirit of the Lord."

As we take time to look into the mirror of God's word, the veil is removed from our eyes. We are then able to lay hold of Christ in all His glory, while at the same time allowing the Holy Spirit to reveal to us who we are. This empowers the transforming ministry of the Holy Spirit to change us from glory to glory and bring us to place of freedom. This is the miracle of the glorious gospel of our Lord Jesus Christ. Paul puts it this way in Romans 5:18-21:

> "Therefore, as through one man's offense judgment came to all men, resulting in condemnation, even so through one Man's righteous act the free gift came to all men, resulting in justification of life. For as by one man's disobedience many were made sinners, so also by one Man's obedience many will be made righteous. Moreover the law entered that the offense might abound. But where sin abounded, grace abounded much more, so that as sin reigned in death, even so grace might reign through righteousness to eternal life through Jesus Christ our Lord."

I love how the Holy Spirit works this process of change and enables us to partner with Him. This is why Equippers is more than a brand for a group of churches that have linked together. It is about function, ministry and mission. We are equipping people for life through faith in Jesus Christ.

I mentioned in a previous chapter how the Holy Spirit called me to be an 'Equipper', beginning a journey of discovery into God's greater purpose. The movement I am credentialed with has historically held a very strong view on the role of the ascension ministry gifts of Christ. The movement, once known as the Apostolic Church, was born out of the Welsh revival at the beginning of the twentieth century. The people in the early days of the movement believed they were called to bring order to the revival, and one of their strong messages centred around Ephesians 4:11:

"He Himself gave some to be apostles, some prophets, some evangelists, and some pastors and teachers."

These early leaders classified the roles of Apostle, Prophet, Evangelist, Pastor and Teacher as the "Headship Gifts of Christ." These were gifts given by God to the church primarily for the purpose of governance, with the gifts of Apostle and Prophet particularly recognised as laying the foundations for others to build upon.

Over time, a constitution was created around this interpretation that, from my perspective, eventually became very hierarchical in function and smothered these powerful gifts of grace from their true biblical function. Throughout my journey, I have come to see these as the 'servant gifts' of Christ, given to the church for its edification, to empower everyone for ministry, and to disciple people towards a place of maturity that reflects the glory of God.

In 1 Peter 5:1-4, Peter clearly sets out the governance aspect of church leadership, stating that even though he is an apostle, he identifies himself as a fellow elder:

"The elders who are among you I exhort, I who am a fellow elder and a witness of the sufferings of Christ, and also a partaker of the glory that will be revealed: Shepherd the flock of God which is among you, serving as overseers, not by compulsion but willingly, not for dishonest gain but eagerly; nor as being lords over those entrusted to you, but being examples to the flock; and when the Chief Shepherd appears, you will receive the crown of glory that does not fade away."

In reality, Peter is setting out the importance of leadership to bring vision and covering to the church. In Ephesians 4, however, Paul is describing function:

"And He Himself gave some to be apostles, some prophets, some evangelists, and some pastors and teachers, for the **equipping** of the saints for the work of ministry, for the edifying of the body of Christ"

— EPHESIANS 4:11-12

According to Strong's Concordance, the only time the Greek word *katartismos* is used in the New Testament is in this passage. In English, it is best translated as a noun—'equipper'—which is an inherent, designated function. This is in contrast to the Greek word, *katartizo,* which is a verb and is about doing. This is helpful in understanding the role of the Ephesians 4:11 gifts.

In his letter, Paul challenges people with these gifts of grace to become 'equippers'. Their function is to restore every person back to God's original design so that immaturity and selfishness would no longer have the power to deceive and rob people of God's purpose. They are instructed to assist everyone to come to the understanding of the importance Christ places on the church. This guards us from living in isolation and means that every believer can be joined and knitted together. The growth and edification of the church happens when we realise our need of one another!

I came to the realisation that through the gifts of grace given to me, my primary function was to be an equipper. As such, I have a responsibility to bring people to a place of maturity, to restore them to God's creative order, to help them understand the importance of church, and to help them see the importance of their contribution.

In contrast, the verb form of the word, *katartizo*, is used a number of times in other parts of scripture to highlight significant actions which illustrate how the Holy Spirit brings change into our lives so we can fully embrace God's path to maturity and be restored to His original design.

As we end this chapter, let's take a look at how He equips us:

1. **Mending.** In Matthew 4:21, Jesus tells the story of two brothers who are mending *(katartizo)* their nets after fishing. A fisherman needs to mend his net because of the damaged incurred by predators ripping holes in them. Through the daily activities of life, the enemy can seek to damage the fabric of our soul through jealousy, offences, broken relationships, the death of a loved one, and many other imposing, often unexpected, forces which seek to tear apart our emotional wellbeing and bring distress to our minds. Through the Word of God and the ministry of the Holy Spirit, we can embrace a process of mending these broken, damaged areas.

2. **Restoring.** In Galatians 6:1, Paul references how to restore *(katartizo)* a person who has fallen into sin. Everyone, at some point in life, falls prey to sin. Depending on the level and nature of our sin, it is important that we have people around us who can restore us so that shame and guilt can be removed, unhealthy habits can be challenged, and mindsets can be addressed with a spirit of gentleness.

3. **Perfecting.** In Matthew 21:16, we read an illustration of how children have perfected *(katartizo)* praise. The praise of a child is pure and uncluttered, and Jesus uses their example to draw our attention to what 'perfected praise' looks like. The Bible also teaches us the importance of praise in ushering in the presence

of God. It is in an environment of praise that the Holy Spirit is able to minister into our lives.

4. **Completing.** In 2 Corinthians 13:11, Paul is explaining his desire to see the Christians become complete *(katartizo)*. I love this application of the word, because Paul is encouraging the Corinthians to keep their sights on becoming complete, just as Adam and Eve initially were in the garden, and to not lose sight of God's complete redemptive plan for their lives.

5. **Framing.** In Hebrews 11:3, the writer highlights the importance of God's word in framing *(katartizo)* the worlds. It's interesting to note that God framed the things that were not evident by what He spoke. He framed (or, created) everything by what He said! The same God that the Bible opens with in Genesis 1 lives and dwells in us. This means that we have the same creative power to frame our future as we speak words of faith.

6. **Joining.** In 1 Corinthians 1:10, Paul challenges the church to not allow a spirit of division to rob them of the blessing that comes from being perfectly joined *(katartizo)* together. Much of Paul's writings in the New Testament reiterate the importance and power of unity. We know from Psalm 133:3 that this is where God commands the blessing. Likewise, Ephesians 4:16 speaks of the whole body being edified as each part is "joined and knit together."

7. **Training.** In Luke 6:40, Jesus directs people's attention to the importance of discipleship and of being perfectly trained *(katartizo)* for the mission given to us by Jesus in Matthew 28:19 to "go into all the world and make disciples."

Each of these verses of scripture give different applications to the same Greek word, *katartizo*. As you can see, an 'equipper' is called to empower people for ministry, so the body is edified, but an equipper also has the responsibility to mend, restore, perfect, complete, frame, join, and train so that every believer becomes the person God originally designed them to be.

David had an understanding of this when he summarised God's design for us with these words:

"I will praise you, for I am fearfully and wonderfully made; marvellous are Your works, and that my soul knows very well."

— PSALM 139:14

PART FIVE

GIFTS AND GODLY ATTITUDES

13

Embrace God's Gifts

God has created every person on the planet with their own unique expression and individual characteristics. If we are to empower people to live out their full potential while staying true to their unique design, we must learn to appreciate and identify the gifts God has placed within each of us.

In the New Testament, there are four key passages that talk about the gifts or talents God has given to people: *1 Corinthians 12:4-7, Romans 12:3-8, Ephesians 4:11 and 1 Peter 4:10-11.*

In 1 Corinthians 12:4-6 (emphases mine), Paul identifies three different functions of gifts:

> "There are diversities of gifts, but the same Spirit. There are differences of **ministries**, but the same Lord. And there are diversities of **activities**, but it is the same God who works all in all. But the **manifestation** of the Spirit is given to each one for the profit of all."

1. Ministry (v. 5). In the previous chapter we looked at the gifts of grace given to the church for the equipping of God's people in Ephesians 4:11-16. They enable every believer to become a

minister, and to fulfil their God-given mandate.

2. Motivation (v. 6). The Holy Spirit has given gifts that determine the motivation or 'drive' of each person. The effects produced by these gifts are the result of the operation or manifestation of the Spirit. The Greek phrase for 'diversities of operations' or 'diversities of energy', carries the word *energema,* meaning 'effect' or 'energy'. These motivational gifts are listed in Romans 12:3-8 and they detail the distinctive God-given 'motivation' each person has. These gifts make each of us unique in our expression and 'drive'. This group of gifts is the main focus of this chapter.

3. Manifestation (v. 7). It is the Holy Spirit's function to reward the use of our manifestation gifts for the profit of all. I often think of these gifts as being similar to the tools in my toolbox. These are supernatural gifts of God given to heal, deliver, and set free the oppressed. It is exciting to witness the manifestation of God's power through these gifts! Paul explains these manifestation gifts in the following verses:

"For to one is given the word of wisdom through the Spirit, to another the word of knowledge through the same Spirit, to another faith by the same Spirit, to another gifts of healings by the same Spirit, to another the working of miracles, to another prophecy, to another discerning of spirits, to another different kinds of tongues, to another the interpretation of tongues. But one and the same Spirit works all these things, distributing to each one individually as He wills."

— 1 Corinthians 12:7-11

Very early in my journey with the Holy Spirit, I learned that there is a difference between the *manifestation* gifts (1 Corinthians 12:1-11) God entrusts us with for the purpose of extending His kingdom, and our *motivational* gift (Romans 12:3-8) which determines our inner passion or 'drive', and is often reflected in our character from a very young age.

In Romans 12, Paul lists the seven motivational gifts as: prophecy, serving, teaching, exhorting, giving, organizing, and mercy. If we are to honour the particular gifting in ourselves and others, it is crucial that we learn to identify these motivational gifts. The reality is that each of us has an innate desire to know who we are, to understand our passions, and to find out what we are called to do. This is a God-given desire. When we understand how God is motivating us, we can better understand the 'calling' on each of our lives. This in turn enables us to achieve a deeper level of self-acceptance and purpose. As we operate in our particular gift, we experience personal fulfilment and a deep sense of joy, and we begin to enjoy 'maximum fruitfulness with minimum weariness'.

There are many tools that are useful in helping us discover our motivational gift (see Appendix). However, when we identify our primary motivational gift, we should not conclude that we cannot exercise the other gifts. The ultimate expression of every gift is personified in Christ. The more we become like Him, the more we will express each of the gifts in a balanced manner. Even so, we will tend to use them from our one basic God-given motivation.

In the end, it is our responsibility to discover what motivates us and which unique gifts God has given to us by His grace. We then need to embrace and exercise our motivational gift.

> "Having then gifts differing according to the grace that is given
> to us, let us use them."
> — ROMANS 12:6

If we attempt to be anything or anyone other than the person God created us to be, we move outside of operating in God's grace. Grace is the desire and ability (or power) to do God's will. When we accept and appreciate the particular gift God has blessed us with, we will experience more of His power in and through our lives.

When Helen and I first began to understand the dynamics of the motivational gifts, it helped us understand one another better, especially in terms of our individual responses. It also gave us insight into each of our children. We would often joke, because our daughter Rebecca has the beautiful looks of her mother but a similar motivational gift mix to me. Helen is very mercy-motivated, whereas Rebecca, in her initial responses, has a prophetic motivation. The benefit of understanding this is that we can establish a greater level of acceptance and appreciation for one another and learn to champion each other's unique gifting.

———

Helen recently published a devotional book called, "Make the Shift." In it, she included two entries that illustrate our different giftings. I hope these will be helpful as you consider your own motivational gift, and pray they will encourage you to go on a journey to discover and stir up the gift God has placed in you.

BOSS IT LIKE BRUCE

"Having then gifts differing according to the grace that is given to us, let us use them . . . (let) he who **leads** (do so) with diligence."
— ROMANS 12:6,8 (PARENTHESES MINE)

Have you ever wondered why some people are just bossier than others? Did they become bossy through practice, or were they just born that way?! God has given some people the grace gift of leadership—and for those people, the latter is true! Because they feel like the boss, they act like the boss, particularly if no one else is leading or taking charge; they just step in to fill the gap! This grace is evident even in a very young child who is able, with ease, to take control of a whole room of people and organise everyone accordingly.

"You bossed it" is an expression we use when someone has done a great job, overcome an obstacle, or succeeded in some significant challenge. It's an affirmation that the person has totally owned the challenge and successfully risen to the occasion. My husband Bruce has such a gift! He has 'bossed' the call of God in his life, planting churches and raising significant leaders around the world. He has owned his responsibility fully by maintaining a willing and yielded spirit. The strength of his gift, as I have observed it 'up close and personal,' is a fearless focus, an inner resolve that doesn't yield to pressure, and a possession of personal confidence—something I aspire to emulate! Bruce's 'take charge' attitude has brought security and ease to my life! I am totally grateful for his consistent encouragement and support, his championing of me to be all that God has called me to be, and for the many practical areas in our life and marriage that he just naturally assumes are his responsibility, things he 'bosses' on an everyday level! That's boss leadership right there!

When this gift and call of leadership is fully surrendered to the lordship of Jesus, it enables the person in possession of it to direct the crowd, discern atmospheres, gauge efficiency, and confront issues where needed with no fear for their own personal safety and wellbeing! They prefer it mostly plain and simple—in other words, clear and uncluttered, with no frills! Their strong conviction enables them to suffer rebuffs, criticism, and persecution for the cause of Christ and the advancement of the Gospel. Bruce's grace-gift operates at a premium in the kingdom of God as he maintains a soft heart towards God and a thick skin toward unfair criticism. He is totally bossing it!

We are all differently graced in our expression of life and ministry, and all our gifts at times need to be tempered for the sake of relationships and effectiveness within the body, or in a family context. At times, the strength of our gift can be 'too much' for the particular setting we are in. For those graced in leadership, discernment is needed to know when to defer and allow another grace gift to come forward—to understand which occasions don't require them to take charge!

"Many roads lead to Rome" is an expression that we are familiar with, indicating there are several ways to get to the same destination, although they may involve different time frames and take different routes. The leadership gift shines in intuitively knowing the best and the fastest route to a destination, or the best and most effective method for a result, but there are occasions where slowing down to incorporate and encourage others along the way is necessary.

I have learned so much from observing Bruce 'bossing it'. His life and faith and his devotion and obedience to the call of God has rubbed off on me, helping me become more confident, decisive, and resilient in my life and leadership. Let's honour the leaders in our lives, give them room to operate, and thank God for those who lead and direct us into all God intended for us!

HEART IT LIKE HELEN

"Having then gifts differing according to the grace that is given to us, let us use them . . . (let) he who shows **mercy** (do so) with cheerfulness."

— ROMANS 12:6,8 (PARENTHESES MINE).

So much wisdom, joy and strength come to our lives when we understand the way we are wired. God has purposefully graced our lives with a gift, an anointed flow that adds value and creates pathways for ourselves and others to experience more fully the freedom of God's work and purpose for our lives. When we appreciate and use this 'grace gift' with faith under the direction of God, it produces supernatural manifestations of the Holy Spirit!

Understanding the strength of the mercy-gift God has graced my life with helped me make sense of the way I thought and felt. Someone with the 'mercy gift' has a natural empathy for others—they feel deeply, and sense when others are hurting or genuinely struggling with life. They carry a tenderness of heart, but along with this, a vulnerability, as they are able to pick up the full range of emotions present in any environment at any one time, whether they want to or not!

This exposure to 'atmosphere' can make us susceptible to fear and anxiety because of the felt responsibility to respond to a need while not always having the maturity or skill to handle it. When feeling under pressure emotionally, the person with the mercy-gift may compare themselves with their strong leadership-gifted friends and question themselves. What is wrong with me? They look so strong and I feel so weak!

But the exhortation to the mercy-gifted person is to use their gift with cheerfulness, not shouldering the responsibility of healing for another as a heavy weight nor viewing it as an inescapable obligation, but as insight to pray, intercede, and release an atmosphere of faith and healing. When we recognise the inherent nature of the grace within, we can operate in the gift of mercy to unlock people and environments!

Learning to appreciate my 'grace-gift' has allowed it to shine as I have brought it in submission to the lordship of Jesus and found freedom to express the desires of my heart through finding my flow in loving . . .

Loving peace. When tempted to feel anxious about responsibility, I speak this simple phrase to my soul: "Just flow from your heart!" My heart is my asset! Bringing 'heart' to situations can shift atmospheres and release the power of God! My constant desire is to walk in peace and then bring God's peace, harmony and reconciliation into the different environments I occupy!

Loving sincerity. Possessing a genuine, sincere love for God and others, in turn creates a safe place for others to confide and divest themselves of secret struggles without fear of rejection or ridicule. My desire is to have a 'crystal clear heart,' a heart that is transparent, approachable, inclusive, welcoming, and willing to help. I love that the mercy-gift within has the grace and power to gather and multiply!

Loving faith. A deep love and dependency on the Word of God searches out revelation to counteract any fear or insecurity. This has given me a strong confidence in the answers contained in the Word of God and in the prophetic revelation of the Holy Spirit to break yokes and open environments to God's love. My desire is to 'unlock hearts,' to release healing, and to witness transformation. This gift within comes with the grace of creativity to enhance environments and release the energy and the passion of the Holy Spirit.

Loving warfare. A desire to defend territory! Possessiveness is both a strength and a weakness of the 'mercy heart,' but when operating in the right spirit and context it has the authority to watch, to discern and shift negative and spiritual forces that seek to invade, possessing the ability to also forecast a 'move of God'. My personal desire is to labour in the spirit, in prayer and in intercession, believing for amazing victories and significant breakthroughs!

14

Embrace Godly Attitudes

Very early in my journey with the Holy Spirit I learned that there is a difference between the *gifts* God entrusts to use to extend His kingdom (1 Corinthians 12.1-11) and the *fruit* that the Holy Spirit wants to develop in our lives (Galatians 6.22-26). I see these as two distinct ministries of God's anointing that we need to be aware of—the anointing *within* and the anointing *upon*.

An illustration of two trees helps us understand these two distinct functions of the Holy Spirit. The first tree is one we cut from a plantation at Christmas-time for the purpose of celebrating the season. Upon this tree we hang decorations, and under its branches we place gifts. These gifts tell us nothing about the quality or condition of the tree; instead, they testify to the giver. This tree is a picture of the gifts God has entrusted to each of us. They are given to empower us to minister for Him to other people, and we apprehend these by faith. They demonstrate the faith of the person but give very little insight into their character or attitudes.

The second tree is a citrus tree which I can see through the window as I write. This tree is producing an abundant crop. It is laden with fruit, and because the tree is in good condition, it produces healthy fruit. The fruit is directly related to the maturity and condition of the tree. In the same way, the fruit of the Spirit is developed in our lives as we embrace the inner anointing. As we allow the Holy Spirit to flow through us, we are changed from glory to glory. This fruitfulness is essential to embracing a life of legacy. The fruit of the Spirit in our lives makes us more attractive to those around us, and we also benefit from our changed attitudes and Godly character.

As a young Christian starting out on my journey of faith I found the teachings of Jesus known as the 'Sermon on the Mount' to be very helpful in this regard. When Helen and I were visiting Israel, we came to the site near the Sea of Galilee where Jesus preached and ministered to the multitudes that had gathered to listen. On the day we visited, the weather was spectacular. As we looked out from the mount over the waters of the lake surrounded by hills and observed the boats in the distance, we allowed our imaginations to run wild as we reflected back to the moment when Jesus stood there and delivered His longest recorded sermon (see Matthew 5-7). I'm sure all who attended would have hung on every word as Jesus spoke about the attitudes that cause our lives to be blessed and overflow with favour.

Jesus' teaching that day is summed up in these words:

> "For I say to you, that unless your righteousness exceeds the righteousness of the scribes and Pharisees, you will by no means enter the kingdom of heaven."
>
> — MATTHEW 5:20

This verse became a key verse for me, unlocking much of what Jesus was teaching. As Jesus continued speaking, He explained that through Him the law would be fulfilled. Therefore, those who walk with Him should live above the law, and their righteousness should exceed that of the scribes and the Pharisees. Grace in no way weakens the law, but the Holy Spirit empowers us to live *beyond* the law.

With this is mind, the beatitudes took on a whole new dimension to me.

By inviting Jesus Christ into our lives, we empower the Holy Spirit to make us brand new from the inside out. Therefore, the overflow is living in the fullness of God's blessing, displaying attitudes that exemplify righteousness, love, satisfaction, peace, joy and a sense of purpose. In fact, to be 'blessed' simply means to experience divine joy coupled with inner satisfaction.

Romans 14:17 states, "The kingdom of God is not eating and drinking, but righteousness and peace and joy in the Holy Spirit." In other words, the fruit of the Spirit is not dependent on external circumstances. It is cultivated and produced when we live a life fully yielded to Christ.

———

"And seeing the multitudes, He went up on a mountain, and when He was seated His disciples came to Him. Then He opened His mouth and taught them, saying: 'Blessed are the poor in spirit, for theirs is the kingdom of heaven. Blessed are those who mourn, for they shall be comforted. Blessed are the meek, for they shall inherit the earth. Blessed are those who hunger and thirst for righteousness, for they shall be filled. Blessed are the merciful, for they shall obtain mercy. Blessed are the pure in heart, for they shall see God. Blessed are the peacemakers, for they shall be called sons of God. Blessed are those who are persecuted for righteousness' sake, for theirs is the kingdom of heaven. Blessed are you when they revile and persecute you, and say all kinds of evil against you falsely for My sake. Rejoice and be exceedingly glad, for great is your reward in heaven, for so they persecuted the prophets who were before you.'"

— MATTHEW 5:1-12

Let's look at each one of these attitudes and how they can bring a positive outcome to our lives.

Blessed are the poor in spirit, for theirs is the kingdom of heaven

When we approach our Father in heaven with a 'poor spirit' or, in other words, an attitude of humility, we experience the divine qualities of righteousness, peace, and joy in the Holy Spirit. It is interesting to note that in the Bible, humility mostly refers to an attitude we have when we come before God. It acknowledges our need of Him, not only because of what He will do for us, but also to access God's grace to live righteously.

C.S. Lewis said, "Humility doesn't think less of oneself, but thinks of oneself less." This state of humility before God restores the broken, fragmented aspects of our lives that were destroyed by sin, back to His original design. Humility says yes to God's grace, God's word, and God's design so that we reflect His glory and experience the benefits of His kingdom. According to 2 Chronicles 7:14, it is this attitude of humility that releases God's healing power:

"If My people who are called by My name will humble themselves, and pray and seek My face, and turn from their wicked ways, then I will hear from heaven, and will forgive their sin and heal their land."

The further a nation moves from God, the faster is the decline of 'right living'. Pride is a slippery slope, taking us away from righteousness, peace and joy. Humility is the opposite; it positions us to be blessed.

Blessed are those who mourn, for they shall be comforted

I realised at the age of twenty-eight when I lost my father to a sudden heart attack that life doesn't always go as planned. My mother and father were born in the same year, and my mum went on to live to the great old age of ninety-seven, so that meant living thirty-eight years without her husband. I was close to my father and valued his influence in my life. At the time of his passing, we were living in another town, so coming to terms with his sudden death, and not being around in the final weeks of his life, definitely took time to process.

This was my first real encounter with deep grief and pain, and also of learning to receive the Holy Spirit's ministry and comfort. Over time, by allowing the Holy Spirit to minister and not suppressing my grief and disappointment, I was able to come to a healthy place where I was able to honour my dad and move on whilst never forgetting him.

One day, while out walking along the beach front, I observed something that helped me understand the working of the Holy Spirit. A blind man was walking along the footpath with his guide dog. While attempting to cross the road in a dangerous place, the guide dog nudged him back from the path of danger. The dog then guided the man about twenty metres down the road toward a pedestrian crossing where they were able to safely cross.

The Holy Spirit is our comforter, our guide and our teacher. When we invite Him to guide us through the valley of pain, He not only ministers comfort—He teaches us how to embark on a path of healing.

Blessed are the meek, for they shall inherit the earth

Meekness is not weakness; it is power under control. The people who learn the ways of Christ and develop this beautiful grace of meekness are the ones who ultimately inherit God's purpose for their lives.

Meekness could be viewed as the 'breaking in' of a wild horse when it is being prepared to draw the carriage for the coronation of a king. The horse is drafted into a corral and taken through a process of rigorous training. While going through this programme, it is treated to quality food and daily grooming, and is cared for in a manner completely foreign to anything it has known in the past. The horse never loses any of its strength through the training; in fact, it becomes stronger. The training is intended to channel its strength for the important role it will undertake.

Moses was taken into the corral of the wilderness so that God could develop the grace of meekness in his life. It was the quality of meekness that enabled him to confront Pharaoh and lead the children of Israel through their very difficult journey. God blesses His people at every stage of their journey, even when there are areas of our character that have not been trained and are not yet fully surrendered to the Holy Spirit. In Acts 7:35, we read how the children of Israel first perceived Moses as a ruler and judge because of his impetuous actions. However, after Moses experienced the wilderness, grace was evident in his life and he was esteemed as a ruler and deliverer.

Blessed are those who hunger and thirst for righteousness, for they shall be filled

Righteousness cannot be earned; it is a gift given by Christ to every believer. Sports players are proud to wear the jersey pertaining to their team, especially if they are representing their country. When each player puts on the jersey, it is expected that their behaviour will represent the values and culture of the team and ethos of their country.

Jesus Christ gives every believer a garment of righteousness and He expects us to represent Him well in the way we live and act. Righteousness can be explained as 'living right'. Passion, on the other hand, best describes a person with a healthy hunger and thirst. In Psalm 63:1, David expresses his passion for God:

"O God, You are my God; early will I seek You; my soul thirsts for You; my flesh longs for You in a dry and thirsty land where there is no water."

David experienced the perils of lust when coveting another man's wife.

He had amassed great wealth and, as a king, he could wield great power and authority. But in the end, he came to a place in his life where it was only God who could satisfy the deep longing in his heart.

The same principle is also illustrated in the account of the twin brothers in Genesis 25. Esau was prepared to sell his birthright to his brother Jacob simply to satisfy his immediate desire for food. In contrast, Jacob saw beyond his immediate need, and sought instead the benefits of 'living right' with godly purpose. Instant gratification often robs people of the lasting fruit and eternal rewards that become the greatest source of satisfaction when living a blessed and abundant life.

Blessed are the merciful, for they shall obtain mercy

Mercy is one of the most amazing attributes of God, and it gives us an understanding of the tenderness of His heart. He knows that each one of us will struggle with 'broken aspects' of our humanity, but if we simply confess our failings to Him, He promises to forgive. Lamentations 3:22-23 gives us a glimpse into the power of His love and forgiveness when it says, "Through the Lord's mercies we are not consumed, because His compassions fail not. They are new every morning; great is Your faithfulness."

Showing mercy allows us to bring a spirit of forgiveness to situations where we have been hurt or wronged. It is an essential trait in every believer's life. In fact, in the Lord's prayer, Jesus said:

"If you forgive men their trespasses, your heavenly Father will also forgive you. But if you do not forgive men their trespasses, neither will your Father forgive your trespasses."
— MATTHEW 6:14-15

Our journey through life is filled with many high moments, but for all of us there will be difficult times when we are faced with an offence—and the challenge to deal with it in a godly manner.

The first occasion I was confronted with an offence came when a group of leaders in a local church sought to undermine my leadership. I had challenged them in an area that was keeping the church from moving forward but they hadn't taken kindly to my suggestion and were having secret meetings together to build their case. After a period of time, this group sadly disqualified themselves before the people because of their divisive behaviour, and one by one they resigned.

I learned some big lessons through this event. However, the greatest issue I had to face was how this event had affected me and what I should do with the inner offence I had taken onboard towards these people. I knew I needed to forgive, but dealing with the pain of the offence took longer to overcome. Every day for six months, I prayed for each of those involved by name, releasing them from my judgment and blessing them.

We can be desperate to receive God's mercy for our own flaws and mistakes, but how easy it is to delay and refuse to give mercy to others. If we want to live this 'blessed life,' we must not hold other people in our judgement. God challenges us to live with a heart of forgiveness, remain open to His love, and receive mercy to help us in our time of need.

Blessed are the pure in heart, for they shall see God

I love the relationship in the Bible between John the Baptist and Jesus Christ. Even though John was slightly older than Jesus, he had profound revelation into Jesus' beginnings, His present, and His future.

> "The next day John saw Jesus coming toward him, and said,
> 'Behold! The Lamb of God who takes away the sin of the world!
> This is He of whom I said, "After me comes a Man who is

preferred before me, for He was before me.""""

— JOHN 1:29-30

Because John walked with a clean heart, he was able to apprehend God's purpose for his own life. But more importantly, John was able to see through the eyes of the Spirit that Jesus was not only his cousin but, in fact, the Messiah! God's prophetic direction for John's life to "prepare the way of the Lord" was found as John projected beyond his natural earthly relationship with Jesus, and beheld Jesus for who He really was.

Many people walk through life with a sincere belief or an academic acknowledgment of who Jesus Christ was and is today, but they fail to enter into the joy of their salvation because they do not behold Him in His glory. This is why our relationship with the Holy Spirit is vital: He not only makes the Word of God come alive, but He also ministers to us by glorifying Jesus Christ.

Blessed are the peacemakers, for they shall be called sons of God

Jesus Christ distinguished Himself as the Son of God by becoming a bridge between the Father and mankind, making up the deficit of our debt of sin through the cross.

"And you, being dead in your trespasses and the uncircumcision of your flesh, He has made alive together with Him, having forgiven you all trespasses, having wiped out the handwriting of requirements that was against us, which was contrary to us. And He has taken it out of the way, having nailed it to the cross. Having disarmed principalities and powers, He made a public spectacle of them, triumphing over them in it."

— COLOSSIANS 2:13-15

There is a big difference between a 'peacekeeper' and a 'peacemaker'. Peacekeepers work hard to suppress actual problems, attempting to mend external issues without dealing with the root causes. Peacemakers, in contrast, are prepared to endure conflict and deal with the root causes because they can see the ultimate prize of enduring peace.

Much effort, money, and time has been spent by peacekeepers attempting to bring stability and reconciliation in the Middle East. Agreements have been drafted between Israel and Palestine, but without understanding the thousands of years of conflict and history these agreements always prove to be very fragile. This happens when all the attention is placed on healing current problems while the root issues are never addressed.

A strong quality of a good leader is conflict management. It is the ability to confront issues and deal with problems quickly. At Equippers we understand the importance of 1 John 1:7: "But if we walk in the light as He is in the light, we have fellowship with one another, and the blood of Jesus Christ His Son cleanses us from all sin." That's why, as a team, our ethos is, "nothing goes under the carpet."

Hidden agendas can breed suspicion and destroy trust, while hidden issues can become a breeding ground of gossip, backbiting, misunderstanding, and discord, eroding trust between people and communities. A *peacemaker* will endure the valley of pain so that clarity and trust can be re-established.

Jesus Christ revealed Himself as God's Son through His life and, ultimately, His death on the cross. We distinguish ourselves as sons or daughters of God when we seek to become a peacemaker in a world where the devil is orchestrating hate, anger, selfishness, covetousness, doubt, and fear.

Blessed are those who are persecuted for righteousness' sake, for theirs is the kingdom of heaven

Righteousness attracts persecution because it exposes the true intentions of another's heart, revealing any internal darkness or hidden desires.

Some Christians have claimed to be persecuted when, in essence, they are being attacked or exposed because of their own stupidity and oftentimes sinful behaviour.

In Romans 14:17, Paul states, "the kingdom of God (or, kingdom of heaven) is not eating and drinking, but righteousness and peace and joy in the Holy Spirit." Both humility and persecution grant us access to these powerful attributes of righteousness, peace and joy, even though they come from opposing sides. The writer to the Hebrews explains it like this:

> "Therefore we also, since we are surrounded by so great a cloud
> of witnesses, let us lay aside every weight, and the sin which so
> easily ensnares us, and let us run with endurance the race that is
> set before us, looking unto Jesus, the author and finisher of our
> faith, who for the joy that was set before Him endured the cross,
> despising the shame, and has sat down at the right hand of the
> throne of God."
>
> — HEBREWS 12:1-2

Jesus gave the same teaching in Matthew 5:12 when He said, "Rejoice and be exceedingly glad, for great is your reward in heaven, for so they persecuted the prophets who were before you."

Over the years I have heard many accounts about the great revivalist, John Wesley. Once, while riding his horse from one destination to another, he found himself contemplating the fact that many days had passed without any form of attack or persecution. He dismounted his horse, knelt on the ground, and began to reach out to God in prayer with words to this effect: "O God, forgive me for my lack of impact." A man spotted him while he was praying and, upon realising it was John Wesley, began throwing stones at him and cursing him for his faith. John Wesley rose from prayer and openly expressed thanksgiving and praise to God because now it was clear that God hadn't left him, and his life was still having an impact.

Every man or woman who stands up for Jesus Christ and His righteousness will most likely be misunderstood and persecuted. May we never take this personally, but see it as a part of the territory of those who live for the cause of Christ and are passionate to see His kingdom advance.

15

Rising Above

It has been a real joy for me to write this book, and to testify of God's grace in my life, as well as telling the story of the Equippers Network. The scriptures I have drawn from have shaped our vision and enabled us to carve out our future, craft our 'today,' and stay focused on the cause of Christ and God's eternal purpose.

When I turned seventy, the Holy Spirit clearly spoke to me that our influence in the future would far exceed everything we had seen to date. He also gave me the following verse as a prophetic prayer to pray:

"... those who wait on the LORD shall renew their strength;
They shall mount up with wings like eagles, they shall run and
not be weary, they shall walk and not faint."
— Isaiah 40:31

According to Strong's Concordance, the word 'wait' comes from a Hebrew word meaning, "to bind together." When I came to this realisation, I was delighted because a strong aspect of my journey has been learning to trust the voice and initiative of the Holy Spirit.

Early on in my journey, Proverbs 16:3 (AMP) spoke powerfully to me:

"Roll your works upon the Lord (commit and trust them wholly to Him; He will cause your thoughts to become agreeable to His will, and) so shall your plans be established and succeed."

When we are totally surrendered to the Lord and in a constant mode of prayer and waiting, the Holy Spirit and God's Word are being interwoven into our lives so that our thoughts and desires come into agreement with the will of God. It's like braiding three strands of rope together—the result is increased strength. For over two years, as I have focused on this scripture as a source of revelation and faith for my praying, I have witnessed my strength growing both emotionally and physically, and also in areas of conviction.

This book is a result of this prayer, because in times past, I have made many excuses relating to my lack of engagement to write. Having dyslexia, writing has never been my strongest skill, but because of three clear prophetic words from people I respect, and a growing conviction and awareness of the Holy Spirit's leading, I set myself to obey.

Learning to mount up with wings like an eagle so we get to see as Christ sees is an important discipline. Life can become very intense, whether because of global difficulties such as the Covid-19 pandemic, or the day-to-day struggles we face in areas such as business, finances, education, marriage and family, other relationships, or health. These are all pressing issues, but in the Bible we are taught how to resist the temptation to be smothered by the fog of despair that seeks to settle and consume us. The Bible teaches us to see ourselves instead as seated with Christ in heavenly places (Ephesians 2:6), and to set our minds on things above, not on things of the earth (Colossians 3:1-20).

I love flying into London (or any city!) on a beautiful day, because from above I can see the whole city from a completely different perspective than when travelling in a car or travelling from one destination to another in the confines of an underground train. Similarly, God allows us to see the view from His perspective as we determine to 'mount up with wings like an eagle' in the power of the Holy Spirit.

When we do that, the promise stands that we will run and not be weary. Weariness is what we identify as 'burnout'. It doesn't matter how much sleep people in this condition have, they constantly battle fatigue, living tired, and often, depressed. Weariness drains our energy because we become inwardly stressed and anxious about problems that we have no power to fix. Seeing our circumstances through God's eyes, however, helps us keep moving forward. We need our faith strengthened so that we can walk and not faint because of lack of progress.

It is my prayer that you will take time to simply wait upon the Lord and allow the Holy Spirit to strengthen your spirit, soul, and body; that you would intentionally set your mind on things above, mounting up with wings like an eagle so that you can see as Christ sees and be able to run the race Christ has set before you unencumbered, walking in faith till the end. Be blessed!

IDENTIFYING SPIRITUAL GIFTS

by Bill Gothard
Adapted by Helen Monk

It is important to understand how God motivates us so we can apprehend the full potential of our life, our marriage, our family, and our place in the Church. To experience this we must have a clear Biblical understanding of the way we are wired. As Paul says in 1 Corinthians 2:1, "Now concerning spiritual gifts, brethren, I would not have you ignorant."

Three types of gifts are portrayed in the Bible:

1. Motivational Gifts
2. Ministry Gifts
3. Manifestation Gifts

People often misunderstand the way they are made because they confuse their ministry gift with their motivational gift. It is our responsibility to identify and cultivate our *motivational gift* and to exercise it in faith. This enables us to impact our world as we align with God's inherent design for each of us.

The motivational gifts take seven distinct and clearly recognizable forms. These are listed in Romans 12:6-8:

Prophecy (vision) | *Serving (energy)* | *Teaching (structure)* | *Exhorting (favour)*
Giving (resourcing) | *Organising (authority)* | *Mercy (empathy)*

We are each gifted in one of these areas. If each of us possessed all seven motivational gifts, we would have no need of other members of the body. 1 Peter 4:10 says, "as each one has received *a gift*, minister it to one another, as good stewards of the manifold grace of God." As we become more like Christ, however, we increasingly express each of the gifts. Even so, we will always operate from one primary God-given motivation.

As you read the following summaries, determine which one best describes you (and those you lead). People with certain gifts are often attracted to working with people with similar giftings. Other gift pairings are more challenging to our relationships. However, it is essential that we do not isolate ourselves from those with different gifts to us. This is especially true in complex situations where utilizing diversity of gifting can facilitate breakthrough. There is a lot to be gained by having greater clarity about how you and those around you are uniquely wired.

THE MOTIVATIONAL GIFT OF

PROPHECY

Biblical Example: Peter
Key Function: 'Eye of the Body' (Perception)
Key Requirement: A clear conscience
Occurrence: 12% of people are motivated by this gift

KEY CHARACTERISTICS

A need to express themselves. Prophets need to express their thoughts and ideas verbally, especially when matters of right and wrong are involved.
Peter spoke more often than any other disciple. He also became the spokesman for the early Church (See Acts 2:14, 3:12, 4:8 and 11:4).

Form quick impressions of people. Prophets tend to make quick judgements based on what they see and hear. They express their views before others speak.
Peter spoke first more than any other disciple (See Matthew14:28, 15:15, 16:16 & 22, 17:4, 19:27; John 6:68 and 13:6).

Alertness to dishonesty. Prophets have an amazing ability to sense when someone or something is not what it appears to be. They react harshly to any form of deception and dishonesty.
Peter reacted harshly to Ananias and Sapphira (See Acts 5:3-10).

A desire for justice. Prophets tend to 'cut off' those who sin so that justice will be done and others will be warned.
Peter asked Jesus how often he must forgive (See Matthew 18:21).

Open about their own faults. Prophets are as open about their own failures as they want others to be about theirs.
Peter said, "Depart from me; for I am a sinful man" (See Luke 5:8).

Wholehearted involvement. Once prophets are committed to a cause, they are quick to respond to opportunities.
Peter asked Jesus to 'bid him to come' (See Matthew 14:28).

Loyalty to truth verses people. Prophets are loyal to truth, even if it means cutting off relationships.
Peter affirmed, "You have the words of eternal life" (See John 6:67-69).

Willingness to suffer for right. Prophets are eager to suffer when it comes to standing for the truth or doing what is right.

Peter and the apostles rejoiced "that they were counted worthy to suffer shame" (See Acts 5:29-42).

Persuasive in defining truth. Prophets have a special ability to articulate right and wrong.

On the day of Pentecost, Peter's preaching brought great conviction of sin, and that day, three thousand were converted (See Acts 2:23).

POTENTIAL MISUSES

- Exposing sin without restoring the sinner
- Impulsiveness; jumping to conclusions (opposite to the 'Teacher' gift)
- Holding onto unforgiveness (more interested in the sin than the person)
- Tendency to self-condemnation (e.g. Peter's need for reassurance in Mark 16:7,8)
- Cutting off people who fail
- Lacking tact when rebuking people
- Dwelling on the negative

CHILDHOOD CHARACTERISTICS

1. Often lack a good imagination.
2. Prefer 'real' activities such as sports; not toy-orientated.
3. Very people-orientated. Dislike being alone; tend to follow mum around.
4. Like stories that contain morals.
5. Only read things that interest them.
6. Usually have understanding beyond their years.
7. Can be negative, easily depressed, and hard on self.

THE MOTIVATIONAL GIFT OF
SERVING

Biblical Example: Timothy
Key Function: 'Hands of the Body'
Key Requirement: Authority
Occurrence: 17% of people are motivated by this gift

KEY CHARACTERISTICS

See practical needs and want to meet them. Important needs that seem insignificant to others catch the eye and attention of the Server. These needs are usually physical. *Timothy's serving ability was noted by Paul, who wrote, "I have no man like-minded who will naturally care for your state" (See Philippians 2:20).*

Free others to achieve. The joy of the Server is not just in initiating tasks, but in knowing that through them they are bringing peace of mind to another person, enabling that person to be more productive in the tasks God has called them to. *Timothy served Paul so that Paul could carry out his ministry (See Philippians 2:22).*

Disregard for personal wellbeing. Because the Server sees the importance of the task and is compelled to complete it, they often disregard weariness and health, and will freely use up their personal assets of time, money and strength. *Timothy had ongoing stomach problems (See 1 Timothy 5:23).*

Difficulty in saying 'no'. As the Server is seen effectively meeting one person's need, other people may ask for similar help. The Server feels compelled to help and therefore finds these requests difficult to decline. *Timothy was asked by Paul to "Come quickly" (See 2 Timothy 4:9,21).*

Alert to likes and dislikes. Servers have an amazing ability to find out and remember the special interests (birthdays, anniversaries, favourite foods etc.) of the people they serve.

Need approval/reassurance. Appreciation confirms to the Server that their work is necessary and is being blessed by the Lord. The Server also desires clear direction. *Paul gave Timothy more praise and precise instructions than any other assistant (See 2 Timothy 1:5-7, 1 Timothy 1:18,19, and 1 Timothy 6:20).*

Likes short-term projects. Servers are usually attracted to tasks that serve an immediate need.

Timothy was urged to maintain endurance, and to continue in the calling he was given by God (See 1 Timothy 4:16, 2 Timothy 2:3).

Feel spiritually inadequate.

Timothy needed to be reminded of his ordination and training (See 2 Timothy 1:6-7).

POTENTIAL MISUSES

- Giving unrequested help
- Engaging in tasks at the expense of time with spouse or family
- Working beyond physical limits
- Easily sidetracked
- Neglecting God-given priorities
- Reacting to overlooked needs
- Resenting lack of appreciation
- Working people around their schedule
- Interfering with God's discipline
- Difficulty in saying 'no'

CHILDHOOD CHARACTERISTICS

1. Good with their hands. Learn to colour inside the lines very easily.
2. Adept at manipulating small objects.
3. Great imitators. Want to pitch in with whatever their parents are doing.
4. Like to help, but need to feel they are being constructive.
5. Not always practical, but have good ideas.
6. Usually have one best friend. Operate best in small groups.
7. Tend to be creative during their teenage years.

THE MOTIVATIONAL GIFT OF
TEACHING

Biblical Example:	Luke
Key Function:	'Mind of the Body'
Key Requirement:	Meditation
Occurrence:	6% of people are motivated by this gift

KEY CHARACTERISTICS

Need to validate information. The Teacher wants to confirm that statements are true and accurate (and that they therefore have spiritual authority).
Luke wrote to 'certify teaching' (See Luke 1:4).

Check out other Teachers. Those with the gift of teaching are very alert to false teachers. They like to investigate a person's background before listening to them. Teachers also assume others will want to know their qualifications before they speak.
Luke began his gospel by affirming that he was an eye-witness and that 'he had perfect understanding of all things from the very first' (See Luke 1:2&3).

Rely on established resources.
Luke related his writings to the other gospel accounts and to the Old Testament. Luke also praised the Bereans for checking Paul's statements against Old Testament scriptures (See Acts 17:11).

Present truth systematically. A Teacher prefers to record events chronologically (whereas an Exhorter is more likely to be more pictorial, less concerned with accuracy in their use of language).
Luke wrote an 'orderly account' (See Luke 1:3).

Gather many facts. Teachers often have greater delight in researching facts than they do in teaching them. However, when teaching they feel compelled to provide as many facts as possible.
Luke's gospel is the longest of all the gospels and includes a lot of information that was left out by the other gospel writers (See Acts 1:1).

Require thoroughness. A Teacher enjoys giving details which are not noticed or mentioned by others.
Luke, in his gospel, gives precise descriptions of events, conversations, circumstances, and physical conditions. He details more names, titles, cities, dates, events, and 'sidelights' than any other gospel writer.

Uneasy with subjective truth. When speaking, Teachers prefer to start with scripture and mention experience later, rather than beginning with stories or experience.

Tend to remain silent until information has been heard, observed and verified.
Luke's silence is conspicuous in the New Testament; none of his own statements are recorded.

Persevere with accepted teachers. A Teacher tends to remain loyal to a mentor or a school as long as any truth remains.
Luke demonstrated amazing loyalty to Paul and his message while Paul was in prison. "Only Luke is with me" (See 2 Timothy 4:11).

POTENTIAL MISUSES

- Becoming proud of knowledge (1 Corinthians 8:1)
- Despising lack of credentials
- Dependance on human reasoning
- Showing off research skills
- Placing the mind and reason above the Holy Spirit's revelation
- Taking teaching to extremes; teaching doctrine outside its moral context
- Arguing over minor points
- Criticising practical applications drawn from Scriptures

CHILDHOOD CHARACTERISTICS

1. Orderly, punctual, faithful in whatever they do. Often have perfect attendance in school.
2. Not easily persuaded once their mind is made up. Can be bull-headed.
3. Like intricate toys.
4. Like to read anything from comics to encyclopedias.
5. May not be the most brilliant students, but have a naturally inquisitive mind.
6. Tend to be loners; Are happy with a book in their own room.
7. Dislike large groups. Usually have one friend.

THE MOTIVATIONAL GIFT OF

EXHORTATION

Biblical Example:	Paul
Key Function:	'Mouth of the Body'
Key Requirement:	Understanding God's Design
Occurrence:	16% of people are motivated by this gift

KEY CHARACTERISTICS

Promote spiritual maturity. The motivation of an Exhorter is to see spiritual growth in others' lives. They are willing to become personally involved to see it achieved.
Paul said "I travail in birth again until Christ be formed in you" (See Galatians 4:19).
Paul declared that he worked night and day to "present every man perfect, (mature), in Christ Jesus" (See Colossians 1:28).

Able to see root problems. An Exhorter can discern the spiritual maturity of another person. The Exhorter is motivated to search out hindrances in the lives of those who are not growing spiritually, and to encourage those who are.
Paul saw the Corinthians as spiritual infants (See 1 Corinthians 3:1).

Give precise steps of action. An Exhorter has the ability to visualize what spiritual achievement looks like for another Christian. They are able to help others understand how they can remove hindrances and develop personal disciplines through which the Holy Spirit can work.
Paul exhorts the Romans to know, reckon, and yield. (See Romans 6).
Paul also told Timothy to flee youthful lusts, avoid foolish questions, and follow righteousness with a pure heart (2 Timothy 2:22&23).

Raise hope for solutions. An Exhorter tends to use examples from the lives of others to help Christians see the potential of daily victory.
Paul used his own life to demonstrate God's grace (See 1 Timothy 1:15).
Paul used the testimony of one church to motivate another church (See 2 Corinthians 9:2).

Turn problems into benefits. Mature Exhorters have learned through experience that God gives special grace during trials.
Paul acknowledged the benefits of the trials that God permitted in his life, and how he matured through them (2 Corinthians 1:1-7).

Desire to be transparent. An Exhorter knows that true growth will not take place where there is guilt. They want their own life to be an open book.
Paul told Timothy that Paul's chief weapon was a clear conscience (1 Timothy1:18&19).

Make truth reasonable. Exhorters tend to explain truth with logical reasoning in order to motivate people to act upon it.

Paul's writings have been studied in law schools because of their logic (See 1 Corinthians 15).

Paul reasoned with the Jews, the Greeks, King Agrippa, and others (See Acts 18:4, 26:28).

A desire to share face-to-face. An Exhorter needs to see the facial expressions of their listeners in order to determine their response and to ensure a positive result. In contrast, those with the 'Organiser' gift are generally happy to remain detached.

Paul longed to see his fellow believers, and used personal examples extensively (1 Thessalonians 21:17, 3:10, 2 Timothy 1:4, and 1 Thessalonians 2:11-12).

POTENTIAL MISUSES

- Keeping others waiting (neglect family because of joy in ministering to others)
- Looking to themselves for solutions instead of the Holy Spirit
- Becoming overly proud of their visible results (may settle for outward conformity rather than an inward change of heart)
- Starting projects prematurely, without completing previous projects
- Treating people as projects
- Sharing other people's private illustrations as examples
- Presenting truth out of balance (may avoid doctrine)
- Setting unrealistic goals
- Giving up on uncooperative people

CHILDHOOD CHARACTERISTICS

1. Always well-liked children.
2. Have positive natures and don't discourage easily.
3. Love large groups. They do well one-on-one, but come alive in large groups.
4. Love to act.
5. Always look for a way to make tasks easier.
6. Extremely jovial, and love to tease.
7. Easily adapt to new situations.
8. Can be slow to understand new concepts.
9. Love to read, but prefer true stories (historical or animal stories are ideal).
10. Tend to use their personal funds rather than saving. Will usually eat treats all at once instead of saving some for later.

THE MOTIVATIONAL GIFT OF

GIVING

Biblical Example: Matthew
Key Function: 'Arm of the Body'
Key Requirement: Ownership
Occurrence: 6% of people are motivated by this gift

KEY CHARACTERISTICS

Discern wise investments. A Giver's motivation is to use assets of time, money and possessions to advance the work of the kingdom of God.

Matthew's gospel has more counsel on wise investments than the other gospels (See Matthew 13:44&45, Matthew 6:33&34).

Sensitive to bad investments.

Matthew recorded the parable about bad investments (Matthew 25:14, Matthew 6:19-21).

Want to give quietly. Givers know that future reward is more valuable than present praise, thus they give quietly and often anonymously. Givers look to the Lord for direction, and they want the recipients to look to the Lord (rather than to them) for provision.

Matthew is the only gospel writer who emphasised secret giving (Matthew 6:1-4).

Give according to God's prompting. A Giver reacts against pressured appeals. They look, instead, for financial needs which others may have overlooked. When they are prompted about a need, they respond spontaneously.

Matthew recorded the words, "I was hungry and you gave me no food . . ." and condemned neglect of the aged (See Matthew 15:3-7 & 25:35).

Desire to give quality. A Giver's ability to discern value motivates them to provide quality gifts; they want gifts to last.

Matthew recorded the gifts given to Christ in greater detail than any other gospel writer, describing them as 'costly gifts' and 'treasures'. He also described Mary's ointment as 'very precious' and noted that Joseph's tomb was 'new' (See Matthew 2:11, 26:6-11, 27:57-60).

Practice personal frugality. A Giver is content with life's basics, and their personal assets are often the result of consistent personal frugality. A Giver is always concerned with getting the 'best buy'. They will put extra effort into saving money and being resourceful with what they have.

Matthew mentioned leaving behind his wealth (Matthew 9:9).

Observe how others use money.

Matthew took note use of Judas' use of the silver (Matthew 27:6&7).

Use giving to motivate more giving. Givers encourage others to give. They want them to experience the joy and spiritual growth that comes through sacrificial giving. Thus, the Giver may provide matching funds or the last payment to encourage others to give. *Matthew related forgiveness to debts (See Matthew 18:21-35).*

POTENTIAL MISUSES

- Hoarding resources for self (lose the 'fear of the Lord' and the joy of giving)
- Using gifts to control people
- Feeling guilty about having personal assets
- Rejecting appeals because of a pressuring tone
- Giving too sparingly to their own family
- Giving to projects rather than to people
- Causing people to look to them rather than God
- Waiting too long to give (need to be instantly obedient to the Holy Spirit)

CHILDHOOD CHARACTERISTICS

1. Friendly, agreeable, full of life (often bubbly), and positive in nature.
2. Conscious of injustice and will speak up if something seems inequitable or unfair (e.g. cheating).
3. Easily corrected; can usually be reasoned with.
4. Extremely appreciative and happy to show it.
5. Energetic and need to be occupied (often active in sports).
6. Would rather play with children than toys. Easily share with others.
7. Faithful, loyal and prompt at everything they do.
8. Dependable (if Givers are in charge, they see it gets done).
9. Participators. They join everything they can and take an active part.
10. Usually leaders.

THE MOTIVATIONAL GIFT OF

LEADERSHIP

Biblical Example: Nehemiah
Key Function: 'Shoulders of the Body'
Key Requirement: Suffering
Occurrence: 13% of people are motivated by this gift

KEY CHARACTERISTICS

Able to visualise the final result. When a major project is given to a Leader, they are able to picture the completed task and what it will take to accomplish it.
Nehemiah articulated the goal of rebuilding the walls of Jerusalem (See Nehemiah 1:2-3 & 2:5).

Need loyalty in their associates. To visualise the completion of a task, the Leader needs to know who is with them, and the resources available. Since the efficiency of their operation depends upon the faithfulness of the workers, they would rather have fewer reliable workers than many they cannot count on.
Nehemiah required oaths of commitment (See Nehemiah 5:7-13).

Ability to delegate. A Leader knows which tasks to delegate and which they must do themselves. The Leader is able to sense which workers need more assistance than others.
Nehemiah delegated the building of the walls, but he retained responsibility for dealing with the enemy (See Nehemiah 4:13).

Endure opposition. Once committed to a task, a Leader is willing to endure pushback from perceived opponents and fellow workers.
Nehemiah endured opposition from foreign representatives and from his own people (Nehemiah 4:8-18).

Make jobs look easy. A Leader has the ability to take seemingly impossible tasks and break them into achievable goals.
Nehemiah broke the huge task of rebuilding the walls of Jerusalem into smaller sections which each family or group was able to complete (See Nehemiah 3:1-32).

Very aware of the finer details. A Leader notices what others might consider small details, but which they know are essential in order for the project to be completed correctly. They also tend to remove themselves from distracting details.
Nehemiah did not get involved in actual building. However, he removed obstacles (such as financial pressures), which could have hindered the workers (Nehemiah 5:1-13).

Able to be decisive. Because Leaders can visualise the final goal, they are able to quickly evaluate requests and situations, and make firm decisions.

Nehemiah was constantly asked by his enemies to meet with them. His decisions not to participate were immediate and decisive (See Nehemiah 6:3&4).

Complete tasks quickly. Before a Leader starts a project, they ascertain and secure the needed resources. They assign workers according to their strengths and weaknesses to ensure maximum productivity.

Nehemiah secured timber from the king's forest before the rebuilding began (See Nehemiah 2:8).

Inspire and encourage workers by expressing approval and praise, along with providing challenges and reproof when necessary. Leaders benefit by being strong in exhortation.

Find joy in seeing projects completed.

When the wall was rebuilt, they finished with singing and rejoicing (See Nehemiah 12:43).

POTENTIAL MISUSES

- Viewing people primarily as resources
- Building loyalty through favouritism
- Using delegation to avoid work
- Being unresponsive to appeal
- Placing projects ahead of people
- Overlooking serious faults in those they lead
- Failing to adequately explain or praise
- Forcing decisions on others
- Leading with charisma rather than character

CHILDHOOD CHARACTERISTICS

1. Able to 'sell you anything you don't want'.
2. Organise everybody (like a sheepdog that never rests).
3. Tough-skinned. Can take a great deal of teasing.
4. Interested in how things work and why.
5. Have a wide range of interests and knowledge.
6. Like detective stories.
7. Constantly write notes to themselves.

THE MOTIVATIONAL GIFT OF

MERCY

Biblical Example: John
Key Function: 'Heart the Body'
Key Requirement: Moral Integrity
Occurrence: 30% of people are motivated by this gift

KEY CHARACTERISTICS

Deeply loyal to friends. People with the gift of Mercy are fiercely loyal and may even demonstrate that loyalty by reacting harshly against anyone who attacks their friends.
When John saw the Samaritan reject Jesus, whom he loved, John wanted to call down fire from heaven to consume them (Luke 9:54).

Need for deep friendships. A person with the gift of Mercy has a nature that requires close friendships characterized by mutual commitment which is often reaffirmed.
John enjoyed a close friendship with Christ. He referred to himself as 'the disciple whom Jesus loved' (See John 13:23, 19:26, 21:7, 20).

Empathize with hurting people. The gift of Mercy enables the recipient to sense individuals who are hurting, and to share their pain. Along with pain, people with the gift of mercy sense the full scope of emotions.
John wrote his first epistle to offer joy, fellowship, hope and confidence, and to cast out fear and torment (See 1 John 1:3-4, 3:2-3, 4:18, 5:13-14).

Avoid decisions and firmness. Those with the gift of Mercy find it difficult to be firm with people because they do not want to offend them. They must learn that greater hurt and offences occur when they fail to be decisive.
When John was faced with denying Jesus, he demonstrated a boldness and decisiveness which caused the Sadducees to marvel (Acts 4:13).

Deeply sensitive to loved ones. The gift of mercy carries with it the ability to sense genuine love. It also means a greater vulnerability to deep and more frequent hurts from those who fail to demonstrate sincere love.
John's gospel and epistles use the word 'love' more than any others.

Attract people in distress. People with the gift of Mercy have a deep understanding of those in mental or emotional distress. They attract those with hurts to confide in them.

When Christ died, He assigned responsibility of His grieving mother to John (See John 19:26-27).

Desire to remove hurts. Those with the gift of Mercy will attempt to remove the source of pain from others.

The message of John's first epistle was for Christians to stop hurting and hating each other (See 1 John 3:11,15).

Measure acceptance by closeness. A person with the gift of Mercy tends to need physical closeness to reassure them of acceptance.

At the Last Supper, John sought out the closest place to Christ and leaned upon Him (See John 13:23-25).

John's need for physical closeness may have also prompted his request to sit next to Christ in glory (See Mark 10:35-37).

Attracted to prophets. The concept that 'opposites attract' is certainly true with motivational gifts. People with the gift of Mercy are attracted to those who balance their gentle love with statements of firm truth (such as those with the gift of Prophecy).

John spent more time with Peter than with any other disciple (See Luke 22:8, Acts 3:1-11, 4:13-19, 8:14).

POTENTIAL MISUSES

- Taking offence
- Becoming possessive (seeking sole commitment, a monopoly)
- Tolerating evil
- Failing to be firm or assertive, resulting in others avoiding necessary repentance.
- Leaning on emotions rather than reason
- Reacting against God's purpose
- Failure to show deference, thinking they are the only one needing closeness
- Closing their spirit to insensitive people
- Giving wrong signals to the opposite sex

CHILDHOOD CHARACTERISTICS

1. Quiet in disposition and speech.
2. Easily upset by loud noises or harsh commands. Prefer quiet surroundings.
3. Have a ready smile.
4. Are cuddly and close to their parents; tend to hang off their legs or clothes.
5. Can be daydreamers in school.
6. Have difficulty understanding and therefore communicating their feelings,

although they may talk a lot.

7. Enjoy fairy tales and romantic stories, or stories involving animals.

8. Have difficulty standing up for themselves. If falsely accused, they remain quiet rather than defending themselves.

9. Gravitate to people that others may not like.

10. Tend to love older people, greeting them by name and being especially kind to them.

11. Co-operate when corrected because they don't want to be rejected, but this can result in feelings of resentment.

12. Are usually followers, not leaders.

Lightning Source UK Ltd.
Milton Keynes UK
UKHW011358210821
389240UK00001B/14